Contents

The Jesus Prayer

All of us are called to pray. In prayer we recognize God as the Lord of our lives. We praise Him. We thank Him. We beg for mercy and forgiveness. We ask Him to answer our needs.

In all of our prayer we come before the Lord conscious of our dependence on Him. We approach Him with confidence, as a child to a loving father or mother.

We are confident and full of trust because Jesus told us to "Ask and you shall receive; seek and you shall find; knock and it shall be opened to you." Jesus also assured us, "If you ask for anything in my name it will be given to you."

Prayer is the raising of our minds and hearts to God.

I have found a simple yet profound prayer is the "Jesus Prayer," or the prayer of the heart. It is one of the oldest, simplest and best of prayers. It can be used anytime, in church, on the bus, while driving, while doing the dishes. It is simply repeating over and over, slowly and meditatively, the Holy Name of Jesus.

In its fullest form it uses the words of the blind beggar in the Gospel, "Jesus, Son of David, have pity on me" or "Jesus, Son of God, Savior, have mercy on me."

William Story, in the prayer book *Praise Him* states: "The best way to say the Jesus Prayer is to sit in as much physical and inner stillness as one can manage and to repeat the invocation over and over, slowly and insistently, fixing the mind directly and intensely on the words of the prayer itself, without trying to conjure up any mental pictures or intellectual concepts. One should pray in this way without strain but with real effort for some length of time at each attempt."

1

Some find it helpful to use a rosary as a kind of timer or reminder for the Jesus Prayer. The Holy Name of Jesus can be used quietly and insistently before or after other prayers, or as we prepare to offer Mass, as we approach Holy Communion, or as we spend some quiet time in thanksgiving.

Prayer, any prayer, must involve our whole being and not just a repetition of words or phrases. The Lord asks us to love Him and praise Him with our total being. How can we use the short repeated prayer in such a way that it is an expression from the depths of our being?

I find that it is helpful to connect prayer with breathing. An ancient word for the brief prayer is "aspiration" from the Latin word ASPIRO, meaning to breathe. As I kneel or sit, I take a deep breath and as I exhale I say "Jesus" or the whole Jesus prayer. Or one can use the seven parts of the Our Father, and pray each of them with a single breath. This can be done a number of times during a longer period of silence or meditation. It could also be done briefly at various times of the day during short spiritual "coffee breaks." The same could be done with the Hail Mary, one of the psalms or other favorite prayer forms.

A recent article in *Worship* magazine says: "The attention to breathing at the same time has the remarkable effect of concentrating our attention so that the prayer becomes also an inward breathing of the Spirit. From a psychological standpoint, breathing is one of the few unconscious, automatic activities that can be done consciously as well. When we give attention to it, we place ourselves in the necessary attitude of relaxation and inward direction that is so conducive to prayer. The same practice could also accompany the many beautiful short prayers that are part of the Christian liturgy."

The Jesus Prayer has been used by saints and contemplatives for centuries. It is a prayer of faith, of surrender to the Holy Spirit who dwells within us and who longs to teach us to pray without ceasing to Abba, our dear Father.

Catholic Schools

I believe in Catholic schools.

I believe that Catholic schools must be continued, strenghtened and supported.

I believe in Catholic schools because I am convinced that an atmosphere of faith must be an integral part of an educational program. The paschal mystery—the passion, death and resurrection of Christ—is the central fact of history. There is nothing really more important than that. Jesus Christ, the Son of God, lived among us, suffered, and died and rose again to share His divine life with us. We are members of the family of God, brothers and sisters of Christ and of one another, and committed to share His life, His love and His truth with the whole world.

We built Catholic schools because we were convinced that in order to have a valid educational system it had to be one which aimed at the formation of the human person with respect to his ultimate goal, the human person who learned the deepest meaning and value of all creation and how to relate it to the praise of God.

We need Catholic schools even more today. A Catholic school is one which must be guided and directed by men and women of faith—parents, teachers, pastors. They create the atmosphere where a child can witness and share in the faith lived in an adult community.

Our schools were built with great sacrifices on the pennies, nickels and dimes of an immigrant people. Today some people question the validity and the prudence of continuing their sacrifice. They wonder if it has been worth all the effort, all the sacrifices, all the money, all the suffering and dedication. Maybe we have forgotten the one thing that makes a Catholic school different: it is a religiously oriented school and its aim is a person of mature, adult faith. This is what links us to the past and gives our schools their unique character.

I believe in Catholic schools because they provide the opportunity for the daily study of the truths revealed to us by God. There are those who minimize the importance of the formal study of religion. I am convinced that religious instruction, given in a sequence and with methods appropriate to the age, ability and development of the child, is an essential ingredient in the education of a Christian. To this date we have not found a viable alternative to the Catholic school in providing such instruction.

I believe in Catholic schools because by far the (greater) majority of the American Catholic people want them. Recent studies indicate that 90 percent of our Catholic people want to continue and strengthen Catholic schools. And 80 percent say that they would increase their annual contributions to the church to sustain the schools.

We have to make some hard decisions. We want Catholic schools. But at the same time we have to decide how we can best use our resources— personnel, money and facilities—for the best possible Christian education of all the people of God.

Here is where all of us have to work together in planning Catholic education for the future. The development of diocesan and parish boards of education is a hopeful sign of the co-responsibility of bishops, priests, educators and parents in the educational mission of the Church.

I believe in Catholic schools because they are good schools. We can be proud of the educational achievement of our students.

I believe in Catholic schools because they provide parents with an opportunity to exercise the right of sending their children to a school of their choice. In the recent debate over sex education and the quality of religious education in the schools, many forget the importance of parental involvement in the education of their own children. The Catholic school cannot do the job alone. The home, the school and the parish together form the community of faith in which the mature, committed Christian is formed.

I believe in Catholic schools because I believe that America needs them. The non-public school provides a healthy competition and diversity in education. Catholic schools can and are offering opportunities for educational leadership.

I believe in Catholic schools because they have been a source of strength and vitality of the Catholic Church in the United States.

We all have to be convinced of the importance and the value of Catholic schools for our children, for our communities and for our country. We need the faith to believe that Jesus meant what He said when He told us to "teach all nations" and "I am with you."

Prayer

During a retreat one "goes apart for a while" as Jesus often did, to spend some time in quiet reflection and prayer. Through spiritual reading, meditating on the gospels, and under the guidance of a retreat master, a person looks at the major direction of his or her life. There are always some areas of our life which need improvement: bad habits, neglect of prayer, failure to give of our time and resources to the poor and the neglected, allowing material things to dominate our lives. At the close of the retreat we make some resolutions to cooperate with the grace of God in following the example of Christ in these areas.

On one retreat I had a beautiful experience which I would like to share with you. I listened to a series of talks recorded on tape by a Trappist monk, Fr. William Menninger, on contemplative prayer. I always thought that contemplative prayer was for a small, select group of people who gave their whole lives to prayer—some Carmelite or Poor Clare nuns, for example.

Father William tells the story of an emigrant family, poverty stricken peasants from a village in southern Europe. They decided to go to America to seek a better life. On the day before they left, the people of the village gave a going away party for them and presented them with some small gifts. About all they had, being poor themselves, were gifts of homemade bread and cheese. But at least the family would have food for the long voyage.

For many days the family was on the ship, cramped in a small cabin. Three times a day they ate the bread and cheese. Toward the end of the voyage one of the children of the family, a boy of twelve, asked the father if he would give him a coin to buy something to eat. He was getting so tired of the same simple fare. The father gave the coin to him and the boy went exploring the ship to see what he could find. After a considerable time the boy didn't return. The father became worried and decided to look for him.

The father had been intimidated by the strange surroundings of the ship. Nevertheless he began his search. After some time he found the boy in the ship's dining room, seated at a table surrounded with food of all sorts: chicken and ham, bread and pastries, nuts and fruit. The father was concerned that he would never be able to pay for all that. He called his son aside and was about to reprimand him when the boy said, "First, here is your coin back. We do not have to pay for the food. We could come here to the dining room any time. It is all part of the price of the ticket."

Father Menninger uses this story to remind us that the Lord invites us to eat at his table, taste of his sweetness—and all we eat is cheese sandwiches! Prayer is a response to God's grace. Prompted by the spirit we lift our minds and hearts to him. We praise him. We thank him, we turn to him for forgiveness. We place our crosses before him.

We all learned our prayers as we grew up. We say our prayers—at least sometimes. But there is a difference between merely saying prayers and praying. Father Menninger helped me to realize that as we make progress in praying we gradually listen more. In mental prayer we turn over in our minds some mystery of our faith and see its application to our lives. We do this when we meditate on the mysteries of the rosary or when we make the way of the Cross.

In affective prayer we open our heart in love and praise and thanks to the Lord our God. But in contemplative prayer we relax while in the presence of the Lord and just listen. We allow Jesus present within us to speak to the Father a one or two word prayer like "Father," "Abba" or "praise." We do that twice a day for twenty minutes or more each time. It is amazing what can happen.

God's People—Called To Serve

As a child I grew up with an awareness of some of the differences between Catholics and Protestants. For the most part it was based on superficial observations and external practices. For example, we went to Mass and obeyed the laws of the Church regarding Friday abstinence. We made the sign of the cross before meals. We attended parochial schools. In recent years I have come to see that while there are fundamental differences of doctrine, worship and practice that divide us, there are many more areas of agreement and convergence.

I use the above as an introduction and point of departure for the main topic of this article—ministries in the Church. Protestants usually call the leaders of their congregations ministers. Ours are called priests. As I was studying for the priesthood this difference struck me. I was preparing to accept a call from God and from the Church. I was to share in a special way in the priesthood of Jesus Christ, who is the "one mediator between God and people" and who offered the perfect sacrifice to the Father. I thought about and thanked God for the unique privilege of standing at the altar of Christ as a leader of the people to join with Christ in the mystery of his passion, death and resurrection.

Lately, there has been a growing interest in the Catholic Church about ministers and different ministries in the Church. A minister is one who attends to the needs of others. A minister serves others.

In the Protestant tradition, the minister's first duty was to preach the gospel and to serve as the instrument through which the word of God touched the heart of the believer.

In the early days of Christianity, the Church fostered and encouraged many ministries which flowed from the exercise of the gifts of the Holy Spirit. St. Paul wrote to the people of Corinth, "There are different gifts but the same Spirit; there are different ministries but the same Lord; there are different works but the same God who accomplishes all of them in everyone. To each person the manifestation of the Spirit is given for the common good." (1 Cor. 12:4-5) Then St. Paul lists some of the gifts of the Spirit and the ministries flowing from them: wisdom in discourse, the power to express knowledge, healing, prophecy, the gift of tongues, teaching, giving money to the poor, exhortation, ruling, performing works of mercy.

All of these were given for the common good, for the building up of the Body of Christ, the Church. The Church officially recognized some of the ministries and installed some of its members in ministries (some of them called "orders"). Thus we had teachers, prophets, deacons, acolytes, porters, readers, and exorcists.

Through a complicated series of historical circumstances, gradually almost all of these ministries came to be exercised by priests or by members of religious orders. People came to think that their role in the Church was to attend religious services, to receive the sacraments, to support those who ministered to others. They did not think of themselves as responsible for ministering to others.

Today there is a great shortage of priests. We are being forced to reduce the number of priests in larger parishes, ask some priests to take charge of two parishes, encourage priests to continue beyond retirement age. Maybe the Lord is telling us something. Maybe the Lord is saying to us: "I am with you. I give my people sufficient graces and gifts to build up the Church, to give it life and strength, to serve the community. Find them, encourage them, support them, train them."

It is the task of the Church to extend the kingdom of God to all people, of every nation, of every race, of every economic and social condition. Every member of the Church is called to do his or her part, to be the hands and feet, the mouth and heart of Christ. Usually this is done in ordinary ways in the family, in the parish, and in the community. Sometimes it is done in more formal or organized ways.

We sometimes call this the lay apostolate. Today we are increasingly calling it ministry. People are exercising ministries in many ways according to the gifts they receive and according to the needs of their communities.

Let me describe some of the ministries that I see.

There are thousands of lay people exercising the ministry of teaching in the Catholic schools and in the Confraternity of Christian Doctrine. I thank God for them. In an extraordinary way they are witnessing to their faith. They are the instruments through which the grace of God touches the hearts of young people. Someone called to my attention two men in a parish who had been teaching religion in CCD classes for fifteen years. What dedication! Some parishes recognize their teachers through an annual installation ceremony. Some parishes give them public recognition at the celebration of Confirmation and on other occasions.

More and more parishes have full time directors of religious education. They are part of the parish staff. They provide leadership for the schools of religion, for the formation of teachers, preparation for the sacraments, adult education and countless other programs.

All of these people—school principals and teachers, religious education directors, CCD teachers exercise a ministry of teaching in the Church. They need our support, our encouragement and our prayers. For their part, they must continually be open to the grace of God, and exercise their ministry with faith and dedication. More than anything else they need to strive toward holiness.

There are many other people who exercise ministries in our parishes and institutions: secretaries, nurses, administrators, trustees, ushers, parish council and board members, lectors, Holy Communion distributors, organists, singers, those who work for the missions, those who clean the church or sew vestments, those who attend to the needy, the poor and the disadvantaged, and countless others.

Some would say that the word *ministry* should not be applied to all of these things. Perhaps they are right. All I am saying is that the Holy Spirit gives many gifts for the building up of the community which is the Church. We need to recognize them, encourage them and help people to see that they are contributing to the growth of the kingdom of God.

Above all we need to see that our work depends upon the grace of God. We need to come before the Lord in prayer as individuals and as groups for nourishment and strength. We need to read and meditate on the Word of God. We need to study and respond to the teachings of our faith. We need to worship God in spirit and in truth.

For so long we have thought that almost all of the ministries in the Church were exercised by the priests and whatever lay people did was to help the priest carry out his work. We are seeing more clearly that all members of the Church are given gifts and are being invited to respond.

I talked with a woman who, under the guidance of her pastor, has served as a spiritual director for several other women. She is a woman of deep faith. She spends a period of time each day with her husband and family at prayer and study of the Scriptures. She has made a thirty-day directed retreat with her husband. People come to her for counsel and advice on their spiritual life. She prays with them and gives them encouragement. Remarkable? Perhaps.

I believe the Lord is calling her to a particular ministry in the Church.

I know two or three men with business experience who left their jobs or who have retired and are now working for parishes as business managers. They take care of all the banking, investments, budgets, financial reports, repairs, maintenance, supervision of janitors and many other details that occupy much of the time of a priest in a large parish. At one time we would have thought that only the pastor could take care of those matters.

I know a number of young men and women who are giving two or more years of their lives as youth ministers. They are doing it for a bare minimum salary or for no salary at all. The impact of their commitment on the lives of other young people is remarkable.

All over the country dioceses are establishing programs for the formation of men who will be permanent deacons. They are ordained for a ministry of service, helping the poor, the elderly, the sick and many others.

I know of a number of parishes where lay people are in charge of promoting good reading material. They set up tables of pamphlets, books, magazines, bibles, and even cassette tapes in the church or parish halls. They use their time and talents to bring the message of God through the printed or spoken word.

There are so many other examples that I could think of: participating in pro-life activities, helping young couples prepare for marriage, encouraging family prayer, training Mass servers, working for justice, offering prayers and suffering for others.

Yes, we have a shortage of priests. But I believe that as a local Church we do not have a shortage of God's grace and gifts. We need to recognize them and use them.

Religious Education

For twenty years I was intimately associated with religious education. In particular, I was involved with the recruitment, training and formation of lay people who generously responded to the call of "handing on the faith" to children, youth and adults in their parishes. Nothing is closer to my heart than this.

I vividly remember how as little as a generation ago lay people often were told that the job of teaching religion was reserved to priests, sisters and perhaps exceptionally well qualified lay teachers. That attitude has changed, to a great extent through the rapid growth of an organization strangely called the Confraternity of Christian Doctrine (CCD).

The Confraternity was actually founded about 1560. It is the Church's official association of lay people devoted to the ministry of religious education. It was developed in this country under the leadership of Bishop Edwin V. O'Hara during the 1930's and 1940's.

In the beginning, O'Hara's main concern was for the religious instruction of children attending public schools. As a pastor in Oregon, he had organized religious vacation schools modeled after similar summer bible schools conducted by the Lutherans in southern Minnesota where he grew up. Children from rural parishes were gathered together for two to four weeks during the summer for intensive courses in Christian doctrine.

The movement was developed at first under the direction of the National Catholic Rural Life Conference. In 1934 a national office for the Confraternity of Christian Doctrine was established to foster the development of religious vacation schools and to develop other aspects of the organization, including lay teachers, grade and high schools of religion, adult discussion clubs, parent educator groups, living room dialogues and parish religious education boards.

13

By 1955 the Confraternity of Christian Doctrine became part of almost every diocese and parish in the country.

The faith, dedication and perseverance of the people involved in parish religious education programs over the years has been truly a gift of God. In recent years, they have been aided by directors of religious education. By their professional training and experience, the DRE's bring leadership, knowledge of resources and direction to parish programs.

Now back to the original question. How does a parish recruit sufficient people to teach in parish religious education programs? Some who have been at it for a long time may feel that others should take a turn. Some feel discouraged by a lack of support. Some believe that they are not adequately prepared. Some run into discipline problems.

I am convinced that the single most important aspect of a parish religious education program, whether in a Catholic school or in CCD, is that it arises out of and is surrounded by and supported by a community of faith-filled, worshiping, caring people. The role of the community is so important that if it is not present no religious education program can effectively exist. A living faith community is the context in which the faith of children, youth and adults can grow and mature.

So the first question is not how do we recruit teachers, but rather how do we as a parish community hand on our faith. The whole parish has to be involved. It is not just a question of setting up classrooms, purchasing textbooks and materials and convincing a group of people to be teachers.

Parents, grandparents, uncles and aunts, brothers and sisters, neighbors and other members of the community make up the environment in which children, young people and other adults come to know Jesus and his Gospel. They are the witnesses of God who loves us, who redeems us, forgives us and heals us. They are the link between a loving God who has revealed himself to us and the person who responds in faith, who turns his or her whole life over to the Lord.

Parish religious education programs must include three aspects: conversion of life, formation in Christian mentality and behavior, and instruction on the truths of the Catholic faith. Unfortunately, we have tended to emphasize religious instruction and to neglect conversion and growth in faith.

Now, religious instruction is important. Young people and adults need to know and understand the truths of faith and our Catholic heritage. But it cannot begin and end there.

How do we hand on our faith? How do we recruit teachers? We must begin with the evangelization and catechesis of adults, that is, the conversion and growth in faith of Catholic adults.

Every parish, in addition to the regular Sunday homily, needs Bible study groups, opportunities for adults to come together to pray, to witness God's gifts in their lives and to grow in the knowledge and love of Jesus. Every parish organization, every Knights of Columbus Council, every board and committee needs the opportunity for retreats, days of recollection.

I believe that in this context no parish will lack for dedicated people who will be available to teach children and minister to youth.

Groups of volunteer teachers cannot be put in classrooms without formation and training. Above all they have to come together to pray, to share their faith and to grow in their relationship with Jesus. If this means that classroom instruction has to be suspended for a time while the teachers are being formed, so be it. Nothing can replace adult growth in faith.

Jesus promised, "I will be with you." He said, "You will receive power when the Holy Spirit comes down on you. Then you are to be my witnesses,...even to the ends of the earth." (Acts, 1,8)

Our Pastoral Center Community

I am at my desk on this quiet Sunday afternoon. It is a cold but bright sunlit day. Last night's light snow barely covers the still green grass. An occasional bird flits about. "Kitty," out house cat, checks in once in a while, curious and aloof. Some reflective music is on the public radio station.

At the other end of the house a group of youth leaders is meeting to talk about the direction of youth ministry in the diocese. This is one of hundreds of such gatherings that take place throughout the diocese to help parish leaders in all aspects of Church renewal and ministry.

Tonight a number of retarded people, with their parents and teachers, are coming in for a Christmas program, prayer and reconciliation.

There always seems to be something going on.

It has been a busy but optimistic time for me, what with confirmations and parish anniversaries, the publication of our financial report, budget hearings, an extensive round of consultations concerning the assignment of priests, parish building programs, regional hearings on the proposed bishops' statement on land and land use, speak-up sessions on diocesan pastoral planning, speaking and praying with various groups, and the ongoing work with diocesan councils, boards and committees.

All of this, it seems to me, is related to the mystery that we are celebrating during these days—the coming of Jesus Christ, the Son of God, into out world and into our hearts.

John the Baptist came to announce the coming of the Messiah and to prepare the way for Him. When the time came he said, "There is one among you whom you do not recognize." (Jn 1, 26)

As we prepare for Christ's coming again at Christmas time, we also need to look around and see Jesus who is already here: in His word, in the Holy Eucharist and all the sacraments, in the poor, the weak, the unloved and in one another.

I have the special joy of celebrating these holy days with the community of people with whom I live and work. As I look back over the past four years, I can say that one of the greatest blessings of my life is that I live with a faith-filled, praying, caring community. There are nine of us: four other priests, three sisters and a woman who prepares the evening meal.

We live together, eat together, pray together, share together, and yes, cry together. We tend the garden, freeze and can vegetables, do most of the laundry, prepare meals, decorate, make small repairs, do the shopping and tend to the other details of the household. In all of this we find Jesus who is already here and who is the center of our community.

Our daily celebration of Mass is the highlight of the day as we pray for one another, our families and loved ones and for the needs of the diocese. Every evening around the supper table we say vespers, taking turns leading the prayers and the music.

Two mornings a week we gather for shared prayer.

We have come to treasure and look forward to these times together.

We have regular house meetings, when we have a special meal together and talk about our growth in faith, the gifts that the Lord has given us and work out any problems or misunderstandings that may have arisen. Some people may question that this really happens, but it does. We remind each other that Jesus is already in our midst, that he must be the center of our lives, the center of our household. This is the meaning of the coming of the Lord.

Advent has been a special time. The chapel is simply but beautifully decorated. The Advent wreath on the dining room table is the focus for the daily scripture readings and prayers calling us to the coming of the Lord and his kingdom. But he is already here.

That is what we are all about. We are here as a diocesan staff to work for the coming of the kingdom of God in our diocese. We are here to be of service to parish communities.

The prophet Isaiah reminds us that without God the world is a desert. It is dry, without life, without hope. He declares, "The earth is utterly laid waste, utterly stripped... The earth is polluted because of its inhabitants who have transgressed laws... All joy has disappeared." (Is 24, 3- 11)

He also prophesies, "The desert and the parched land will exult; They will bloom with abundant flowers, and rejoice with joyful song. They will see the glory of the Lord. He comes to save you. Then will the eyes of the blind be opened, the ears of the deaf be cleared; then will the lame leap like a stag, then the tongue of the dumb will sing. Streams will burst forth in the desert." (Is 35, 1-6)

What community living has taught us is that we need one another. We have come to understand that we are weak, but that the Lord uses us in our weakness. He gives each of us gifts that we need to share to build up and strengthen one another and his people.

We don't want to be weak. We want to be in control. We don't want to be dependent on one another. Yet some of the greatest things happen to us when we are weak, when we are sick or depressed, or when tragedy touches our lives, when we accept our weakness and dependence.

Jesus came in weakness as a human being. He taught us that he needs us. Yes, he uses us, weak as we are, to witness to others, to lift up, support and care for one another.

We celebrate the good news that God loves, that he sent his Son to offer us the greatest gift—eternal life. Wow! Isn't that great. Praise the Lord. He calls us to be his children. We can call God "our Father." Jesus is in our midst. He wants to be the center of our lives, of our families, of our communities, of our diocese.

This is my Christmas prayer for all of you: May Jesus take flesh and be real in your lives. May he bless you with his love and his gifts. And may you be open to receive him.

God bless you all.

Future Structuring of Parishes

The Task Force on Parishes is finishing its work. For two years a group of dedicated people, representing the Priests' Council, Diocesan Pastoral Council, Sisters' Council, Pastoral Administrators, Council of Catholic Women, Diocesan Planning Committee, Personnel Committee, Priests' Personnel Board and the diocesan staff, has been meeting with me to devise a plan for the future structuring of parishes in the diocese.

Every family, every person in the diocese will be affected by the diocesan plan for parishes.

It has been clear for a long time that every parish would not be able to have a resident priest. Priests began serving two parishes. Priests were taken from special ministries (religious education, educational administration, schools, youth ministry, hospital ministry, etc.) and assigned to parishes. This diocese pioneered the use of pastoral administrators. Our parishes continue to be served by dedicated, competent leadership.

We need to face the fact that our priests have been heavily burdened. They cannot continue to add to the number of parish masses to offer, meetings to attend, and programs to be personally involved in. In 1978 we had ninety-three active priests. We have seventy-five now. By 1995 we can plan on no more than sixty active priests. At the same time we have seen a remarkable growth in the number of pastoral administrators and other parish ministers.

The question addressed by the task force was: How will we continue to provide leadership in our parishes in 1995 and into the twenty-first century?

The diocesan plan will call for most of the parishes to cluster, that is, to work cooperatively with a neighboring parish or parishes. That will mean a conscious effort on the part of parishes to work together in scheduling masses, celebrating Holy Week, Confirmation and other liturgies, operating a Catholic school, conducting religious education programs, collaborating in sacramental preparation, in adult education, youth ministry, charity and social concerns. No pastor or pastoral administrator should have to work with more than one parish council or one set of parish committees.

Every parish in a cluster needs to have the equivalent of one full-time staff person (ordained or non-ordained). If a parish is not able to support a full time parish worker (a pastoral administrator or a parish staff person), it needs to think seriously about consolidation.

Some parishes will consolidate, that is, they will begin a process of merging two or more parishes into new parish corporations. Given the deep emotional ties that we have to individual parishes, working together and joining together will be difficult. Still, I hear many people saying, "We have been talking about this for a long time. We know that changes have to be made. Let's get at it."

The task force has now presented me with its final recommendation, the result of two years of study and consultation. It is now the "diocesan plan for parishes" and the policy of the diocese. It will be implemented by the Priests' Personnel Board, all diocesan staff, all priests, pastoral administrators, parish councils, and parish and diocesan committees.

It will need the support and commitment of all of us.

Fasting

We modern Christians have lost the spirit of penance and self denial. We Americans have so much. All our needs and desires are catered to. We think that we have a claim on abundance, rich food, big cars, fancy clothing, lovely homes, expensive vacations, and plenty of leisure and entertainment.

I confess that this same spirit has entered my life. I am affected by it. I have to reject that spirit. I have to let Jesus Christ be the center of my life. Everyday I must say, "You are my Lord. I want to follow you. I want to do your will."

During Lent the Church calls us to repentance. As we come to receive the ashes on our foreheads we hear the words of Jesus as he began his public ministry: "This is the time of fulfillment. The reign of God is at hand. Reform your lives and believe in the gospel." (Mk. 1:15)

This is a constant theme of the Christian message. Jesus called his disciples and he calls us to change our lives, to repent of our sins, to take up our cross and follow him.

Jesus said, "Unless you repent you shall all likewise perish." (Lk. 13:3) "Take my yoke upon your shoulders and learn from me, for I am gentle and humble of heart...my yoke is easy and my burden light." (Mt. 11:29-30) Whoever wishes to be my follower must deny his very self, take up his cross each day and follow in my steps." (Lk. 9:23) "Anyone who does not take up his cross and follow me cannot be my disciple." (Lk. 14:27)

The message is clear. We are all called to repentance. We are called to do penance. One of the time-honored methods of doing penance is fasting.

As Jesus began his public life he was led by the Spirit into the desert where he fasted for forty days and forty nights. (Mt. 4:1-2) In imitation, the

Church calls us to fast during the forty days of lent. We are invited to do it willingly, freely accepting the invitation of Jesus to conversion of life and voluntary penance.

I discovered the power of fasting a few years ago. I was on a team of people conducting a weekend Cursillo. I received letters of support from people who told me that they were praying for me and the team during the weekend. Several said, "I offer two days of fasting," or "I will fast one day a week for the next month," or "I will fast for a whole day without any food at all." I really felt the power of that penance. I was deeply moved by the loving concern. I have written similar letters to people. They told me how much they meant to them.

When I came to New Ulm, many people told me that they would pray for me. Some said that they would fast. One wrote to tell me that she was fasting for a week for me. Such a thing does something to you.

Fasting means that we freely deny ourselves in our eating or drinking. It can be done in many ways. The traditional fast in the Church involves eating only one regular meal a day with two lesser snacks. Another way is to fast from all food for twenty-four hours. One could fast by eating nothing between meals. This is a common way to fast and is a restriction on habitual nibbling. Another way is just to eat less or to refrain from something that we really like such as desserts, drinking, going out to eat.

Fasting brings the soul to do the will of God. It opens us to listen to the word of God. Fasting helps us to be under the power of God and not under the power of food. I tell my stomach when to eat; my stomach does not tell me when to eat.

Jesus tells us so clearly to give to the poor, to pray and to fast with the same purity of intention. That is, we do it not to attract attention but out of love of God. He says, "When you fast (he doesn't say if you fast), you are not to look glum as the hypocrites do. When you fast, see to it that you groom your hair and wash your face. In that way no one can see you are fasting but your Father who is hidden; and your Father who sees what is hidden will repay you." (Mt. 7:16-18)

"Fasting is not a substitute for anything else but nothing else is a substitute for fasting. Fasting does not change the will of God but it brings you into a place where you can experience things that are in the will of God that you could not otherwise experience." (Derick Prince)

By fasting a person can put himself in a condition where God can work in him. It helps us to see our dependence on God. It is a humbling process; we can see ourselves more clearly as we really are.

Although fasting is done individually and in silence there is also a time to fast in community. We gain strength and support from one another. I believe that such a time is now, when fasting is at such a low ebb in the Church. We should tell one another when we fast in order to give encouragement to each other.

St. Paul said, "We preach Christ crucified—a stumbling block to Jews and absurdity to Greeks; but to those who are called, Jews and Greeks alike, Christ, the power of God and the wisdom of God." (I Cor 1:23-24)

The cross of Christ seemed foolish to the people of his time. But it has become a banner of hope and a sign of our faith. Doing penance for our sins, fasting and abstinence have become foolishness in our day. But they are a source of strength and power. They open us to listen to the Lord. They put bodily comfort in its true perspective. They unite us to the suffering and death of Christ.

Spiritual Renewal

We hear much these days about "being born again." Actually, such is at the very heart of Christianity. Jesus told us that unless one is born anew he cannot enter God's kingdom.

Our membership in the family of God needs continual renewal. "Reform your lives and believe in the gospel," (Mk. 1,15) Jesus proclaimed. And St. Peter echoed these words when he told the crowd that had gathered at the first Pentecost: "You must reform and be baptized, each one of you, in the name of Jesus Christ," he said, "that your sins may be forgiven; then you will receive the gift of the Holy Spirit." (Acts 2,38)

"Born anew," "spiritual renewal," "conversion," "reform." What does it all mean? What does it mean to me? I used to be upset with people who spoke in such terms. They would confront me with such questions as, "Have you been saved?" "Have you accepted Jesus as your savior?"

I would respond with, "Of course I have been saved. Jesus died for my sins. I was baptized. I am a Catholic."

However, in recent years I have come to understand more clearly that conversion is a life-long process, that I need to be continually initiated into the Church. (Hence, we have three sacraments of initiation: Baptism, Confirmation and Holy Eucharist.) Every day I have to declare at Mass: "Yes, Lord, You are MY Lord. I offer everything to you through your Son Jesus Christ. Amen. Yes."

Whereas it used to bewilder me, it now makes sense when I see people coming forward at the call of Dr. Billy Graham to commit themselves and their lives to Jesus. The Lord uses the faith and the example of other people to move us by his grace to respond to him.

25

If anything is clear in the Church today it is that all of us are called to spiritual renewal. Simply put, that means that our relationship with God needs to be strengthened and made new.

I know that I need proper food and enough rest and exercise to maintain my physical strength and vitality. I realize also that I must spend time and share myself with my family and friends to keep alive our human relationships. In the same way I need to be open to and nourish the "life in the Spirit" that the Lord invites me to.

"I call you friends," Jesus said. "It was not you who chose me, it was I who chose you." (Jn. 15, 15-16) He prayed, "Father, to them I have revealed your name, and I will continue to reveal it so that your love for me may live in them, and I may live in them." (Jn. 18,26)

Imagine. The very life of God in us! That is what we are called to. At Confirmation we pray, " Pour out the Holy Spirit upon them to strengthen them in their faith and anoint them to be more like Christ the Son of God."

That is what the renewal of the Church is all about. We are the Church. We are called to be more like Christ. Renewal is the work of the Holy Spirit and it has to begin with me, with each of us. We have to take time to KNOW him. Not just learn about him and his teachings. That is important, but, we have to KNOW him, to experience him. "Learn of me," he said. "Take up your cross and follow me." "Eat my flesh and drink my blood." "Forgive one another." "Live in me." "Live on in my love."

Church renewal is often confused with the reform of structures in the Church. The exterior framework somehow ought to conform with the nature and mission of the Church. For example, the Body of Christ is made up of many members, each with gifts and called by God to worship, to share the good news and to love each other. So we organize committees, boards, councils and commissions. We hire staff people and recruit volunteers. We reorganize. We print bulletins, newsletters and posters. We call meetings, conferences, conventions and workshops.

All of this may be needed, but it might not be renewal. Renewal has to be first of all spiritual renewal. We cannot organize the kingdom of God into people's lives. All the religious education classes in the world will do little lasting good unless parents and teachers show by what they are and by what they do that Christ is the center of their lives. Members of parish and diocesan boards must first of all listen to the Lord, be in tune with his message, and worship him in spirit and in truth before they can provide any effective leadership.

There are so many signs all around us that the Holy Spirit is renewing his people. People are opening their Bibles, attending Bible study and Bible sharing groups. They are interested in prayer and are saying, "Teach us how to pray." The liturgy—the Mass, the sacraments and the public worship of the Church—is becoming more meaningful to many. Retreat centers are crowded. Married couples are rediscovering that their love is empty unless God is the third party in their relationship. None of this is new, but people are finding it anew.

Personally, I have found three movements especially helpful in leading people to a spiritual renewal in their lives: the Cursillo movement, the Charismatic renewal, and Marriage Encounter.

Involvement in the Cursillo movement begins with a three-day Cursillo weekend from Thursday evening through Sunday. "Cursillo" means a short course in Christian living. The weekend is presented by a team of lay persons and priests. It includes talks, discussion, recreation, song, prayer, reflection, silence and opportunities for Mass and the Sacraments. It is a workshop in the fundamentals of the Catholic faith where everyone learns by experiencing a living community.

The Cursillo weekend can and usually does have a powerful effect on a person's life. In my own case I experienced in a powerful way that Jesus is my friend. He loves me. He chose me. It is ten years now since I drove to Iowa with four other men to make a Cursillo weekend. It is still vivid in my memory. Thousands of others have had the same experience. We come to see that our response to the call of God has to be renewed every day of our lives.

Men and women make the Cursillo separately. It is open to priests, religious, single people and married couples. In the case of couples, the husband makes the Cursillo first before the wife can make it.

The Charismatic renewal is sweeping the country. It is leading people to prayer, to the reading and reflection of the Bible, to a conversion of life, to an openness to the gifts of the Spirit. As a new movement it needs guidance, it needs leadership, it needs maturity. But I have found it to be one of the greatest blessings of God in our time.

Marriage Encounter is a renewal of the relationship of husband and wife. In a beautiful and non-threatening way it brings couples together. Above all it helps them to communicate with one another, and to share their deepest feelings.

"Unless you are born again..." This is the Lord's call.

Diocesan Mission Statement

One of the most powerful religious experiences in my life occurred during the two years in which I studied theology in Rome in 1964-1966. The Vatican Council was in session. Theology is "faith seeking understanding" and faith demands that by God's grace one entrusts his whole self freely to God. It is a total surrender to God: mind, heart, will and body. As I sought to understand my faith, it was strengthened through theological study.

What is more, I saw the Christian message so much more clearly. I saw the central message of the Gospel as something that could be expressed in just a few words, each of them filled with meaning and depth.

God loves me. He has shared his love with me. He has shared his truth with me. And he demands from me a total response in loving surrender, in service to him and to my neighbor. Truth, life, love, response. To me that contains it all. It summarizes all of salvation history, the life of Jesus, the creed, the sacramental mysteries, the commandments, the beatitudes, the whole Christian life.

As I studied the Vatican Council, Sacred Scripture, and subsequent documents from Rome, from theologians, and other sources, the same three ideas kept repeating themselves: truth, life, love. These three, it seemed to me, expressed so clearly the essential mission of Christ and therefore of his Church.

Jesus said, "I am the way, the truth and the life." (Jm. 14,6) By what he is, and by what he says and does, he teaches us all truth. He shares his divine life with us, inviting us into union with him, so that as members of the family of God we can call God our Father and our fellow Christians brothers and sisters. He calls us to follow his way, loving and serving God and one another.

In the document on Revelation, the Vatican Council declared, "Now what was handed on by the Apostles includes everything which contributes to the holiness of life, and the increase in faith of the people of God; and so the Church in her teaching, life, and worship, perpetuates and hands on to all generations all that she herself is, all that she believes."

While I was in Washington, D.C., serving as Director of the Department of Education for the United States Catholic Conference, I was involved in preparing the consultation for the Bishops' pastoral letter on Catholic Education, "To teach as Jesus did." As that work gradually unfolded, these three ideas again came forth and became the theme that bound the whole document together. It says, "Catholic Education is an expression of the mission entrusted by Jesus to the Church he founded...The educational mission of the Church is an integrated ministry embracing three interlocking dimensions: the message revealed by God (didache) which the Church proclaims; fellowship in the life of the Holy Spirit (koinonia); service to the Christian community and the entire human community (diakonia)."

In parishes where I have served and in parishes throughout the diocese of New Ulm we say to our people, "The Church is the people of God. All of us are called by God to extend the kingdom of God. We are to be a community of praying, believing, worshiping, loving people. Jesus invites us to take an active part in his mission."

We encourage the formation of parish councils. And what are the committees that we form to involve people in the mission of the Church? An education committee or board, a worship committee, and a community service committee. (We also have a budget and finance committee, a maintenance committee, etc.)

People in the Church are given gifts by the Holy Spirit to exercise ministries: a ministry of teaching, one of the many ministries connected with prayer and worship (readers, servers, musicians, ushers, communion distributors, decorators, vestment makers, pray-ers) or a ministry of service

(healers, visitors of the sick, those who work for the missions, the poor, the widows, the elderly, for social justice.)

What we always need to remember is that the mission of Christ and his Church is primarily a work of the Spirit. We cannot organize God or a response of faith into people's lives. No number of boards, committees, programs or staff people, no matter how highly organized will of themselves extend God's kingdom. We have to come together first of all to pray and to fall before the Lord. We have to study his message. Gradually we will come to see the needs in our own communities. We expectantly believe that he will give us the gifts to meet those needs. The gifts are expressed in ministries of the word, ministries of worship and ministries of service.

I really believe that this is the way the Lord is calling us to renew his Church. He is calling us to holiness and to develop a personal relationship with him, and through him a Spirit-filled relationship with one another. He said, "When the Holy Spirit comes down upon you, you will receive power; then you are to be my witnesses...even to the ends of the earth." (Act 1,8)

The Kingdom of God

How often as a child I heard the words, "the kingdom of God" as the pastor proclaimed the Gospel. The kingdom of God is like a mustard seed, like the yeast in a dough, like a woman who lost a coin and swept the house until she found it. Jesus so often spoke of the kingdom of God, the reign of God.

As a youth I thought of the kingdom of God as heaven where God reigned and where the angels and saints gathered around His throne.

I knew as a young priest that Jesus said "the kingdom of God is within you." I knew that it referred to the life-giving grace of God which makes us holy.

Frequently as a priest I spoke of the kingdom of God as the Church, begun by Jesus Christ with a small band of followers and destined to spread throughout the world. I quoted Pope Pius XII who said "the Church has no other reason for its existence than to extend the kingdom of God to people of every nation, of every age, of every social and economic condition."

Now all this is true. The kingdom of God is in heaven, it is in the hearts of people, it is found in the Church. But I missed the idea that tied all this together.

I read an article and listened to a series of tapes by Father Richard McBrien, a theologian with whom I studied in Rome. His explanation of the kingdom of God is so clear and helpful that I want to share it with you.

The kingdom of God is wherever God's will is at work. It exists wherever God's power is making love, reconciliation and healing possible.

Fr. McBrien defines the kingdom of God as "the redemptive presence of God." "This redemptive (or saving) presence" he writes, "can be found in everyday personal experiences. Whenever people love one another, forgive one another, bear one another's burdens, work to build up a just and peaceful community, God's redemptive and liberating presence is being manifested."

The mission of Jesus, his very purpose, was to begin God's reign, precisely because he came to do God's will. He allowed the Father to reign in his heart and life completely. "He humbled himself, obediently accepting even death, death on a cross!" (Phil 2,8) He invites us to follow. "Take up your cross and come after me."

"Seek first his kingship over you, his way of holiness, and all these things will be given you besides." (Mt 6, 33) He said, "This is how you are to pray: Our Father in heaven,...your kingdom come, your will be done on earth as it is in heaven." (Mt 6, 9-10)

Doing the will of God! Letting God reign over your lives. That is where the kingdom of God is.

Evangelization And Catechesis

It is my firm conviction that the key issue in the catechesis of children and youth is the catechesis of adults.

Indeed, the most pressing need in the church is the evangelization and catechesis of adults. As the *General Catechetical Directory* so forcibly reminded us all, "catechesis for adults, since it deals with persons who are capable of an adherence that is fully responsible, must be considered the chief form of catechesis." (n. 20)

One could therefore build a strong case for concentrating more of our attention on the evangelization and catechesis of adults as high priority for the Church today. Here I am speaking of the need for adult catechesis insofar as committed, faith-filled adults form the context in which the catechesis of children and youth takes place.

Children and youth look to adults—parents, teachers, the extended family, pastors, the whole Christian community—for models of Christian life and commitment. But so many Catholic adults are inactive in the practice of their faith or simply do not participate anymore. Worse, vast numbers, while continuing to attend church services and fulfill minimal observance of church membership, have never really been converted. They have never turned their lives over to the Lord.

A living faith is the response of the total person, under the grace of God, to the living Word of God. It is the surrender of oneself, of one's life, one's heart, one's hands and feet to the Lord Jesus.

Being born again is at the very heart of the Christian life. Jesus said, "No one can see the reign of God unless he is begotten from above." (John 3:3) Again, "I solemnly assure you, no one can enter into God's kingdom without being begotten of water and Spirit." (Acts 2:38)

Peter echoed these words when he told the crowd that had gathered at the first Pentecost: "You must reform and be baptized, each one of you, in the name of Jesus Christ, that your sins may be forgiven; then you will receive the gift of of the Holy Spirit." (Acts 2:38)

"Born again," "conversion," "reform," "turning our lives over to Jesus the Lord"? Where do we see it? How can children come to Jesus unless they see living witnesses? How can the grace of God touch their lives unless they are immersed in a faith-filled, worshiping, serving community?

We are all called to spiritual renewal. We need to really believe what Jesus promised before he ascended to the Father: "You will receive power when the Holy Spirit comes down on you; then you are to be my witnesses in Jerusalem, throughout Judea and Samaria, yes, even to the ends of the earth." (Act 1:8)

Children and youth need witnesses.

There are stages in the process of coming to a mature, adult faith. First, under the grace of God and the witness of other believers, people come to an initial faith. They accept Jesus as Lord and Savior and at least in a general way respond to the good news that God loves us, that through the death and resurrection of Jesus he has shared his divine life with us and that he calls us to union with him. We call this evangelization.

Then comes catechesis, which presupposes this initial faith and is concerned with nurturing it, strengthening it and making it mature.

Theology, a further stage, is faith seeking understanding, the systematic and scientific investigation of the truths of faith.

In the past several generations we have made catechesis chiefly a matter of religious instruction. And we have made religious instruction a kind of cut-down version of a theology course. We have neglected the central goal of catechesis which is to strengthen faith. And we have almost totally ignored the evangelization of Catholic people, presuming that the initial conversion had taken place in a Christian society.

In ages past, faith sharing was done through the parish, through a community which reinforced Christian values and beliefs, and through the family. We need to work toward building up this sort of faith community again.

Therefore I say that the key to the catechesis of children and youth is the catechesis of adults. Young people need adult witnesses, people who express their beliefs in their daily lives by what they do and say and love.

Giving Gifts

Christmas is a time for giving. More than any other time of the year our thoughts are directed toward gift giving during the Christmas season.

We exchange gifts because we celebrate the greatest present in history when our loving Father sent his only Son to be with us as Savior, Prince of Peace, as Mediator, as Lord. "Yes, God so loved the world that he gave his only Son, that whoever believes in him may not die, but may have eternal life." (JN 3:15) "The gift of God is eternal life in Christ Jesus our Lord." (Rom 8:23)

It is too bad so many of us forget this central fact of Christmas. We exchange gifts. But we forget to relate that giving to the Lord. We give (and maybe expect to receive) gifts that are much too expensive. We look in vain for unusual gifts for people who seem to have everything. We exchange gadgets and appliances (they seem to come up with new ones every year) that are wasteful, energy consuming, and go unused for the rest of the year. We forget the poor.

Jesus said to the Samaritan woman at the well, "If only you recognized God's gift." (JN 4:10) If only we would recognize the gift of God. He gives us Jesus and invites us to accept him, to really believe in him and let him be the Lord of our lives. So simple, yet so profound.

One of the readings of the Christmas liturgy says, "The grace (gift) of God has appeared, offering salvation to all men." (Titus 2:11) And again the scriptures say, "The gift of God is eternal life in Christ Jesus our Lord." (Rom 8:23)

Jesus came to "give himself for our sins." (Gal 1:4) That is what Christmas giving is all about. We give to others in imitation of an all-loving God. We give because Jesus gave himself "totally to us, even to death on the cross."

We value gifts in proportion to the thought and affection that they represent. I remember so well one of the most appreciated gifts I ever received. As a seminarian I taught a group of junior high school students in a CCD program. A bond of affection built up among us. At the end of the year they gave me a set of cuff links. I wore those cuff links for years until I lost one of them. I still have the other one. I looked for a long time without success for a replacement. There was something about that gift that no amount of money could replace.

We value gifts that are homemade, ones that in such a tangible way express the life and love of the giver.

We know that a gift is appreciated when it is used. Isn't it fun when we see someone wearing a shirt or tie or sweater that we gave them? Isn't it a good feeling to know that what we gave was useful, helpful and enjoyed.

Think of all the things God has given to us. He gives them to us to draw us closer to one another and to build up and strengthen his people, the Church. St. Paul wrote, "We have gifts that differ according to the favor bestowed on each of us." (Rom 12:6) Again "there are different gifts but the same Spirit. To each person the manifestation of the Spirit is given for the common good." (1 Cor. 12:4-7)

This message has been brought home to me in a powerful way. Practically everywhere I have gone I have encouraged people to be open to the gifts of God and to use them to serve or to minister to others.

Father Paddy Colleran, a close friend of mine and the national chaplain to Marriage Encounter, wrote just a few days before his tragic death in 1977, "We must have a sense of wonder and belief in these gifts that are ours. We cannot allow ourselves to let these gifts become THINGS. They are WE living our sacramental love. The greatest charism the Lord has given to his Church are the Sacraments. They are the ultimate charisms in the world. We must let ourselves hear deep in our hearts that we are the medium; we are the message; we are the Church."

I received a letter from a woman in Minneapolis who is using her gifts to serve others. I am sure she won't mind my sharing it. She wrote, "It was a cold sleeting November afternoon. My assignment was to go to Branch II of Catholic Charities, which ministers to the street people of Hennepin Avenue.

"As I entered, I was somewhat afraid. Approximately thirty men were there, some sleeping off hangovers, others sleeping, some playing checkers and cards. My question: what do I do? How can I minister? I asked Barb, the girl in charge, what I could do. Her response was, 'Do you play cribbage?' 'Yes,' was my answer as I recalled my father teaching me to play cribbage one winter when we didn't have electricity.

"So I did; it only took a little time and I was in the game. For the next two hours I played. It was four handed cribbage, but by the end of two hours other men had gathered to watch the game. They served me coffee and seemed concerned about my comfort.

"Then I began to see. Just my presence was needed, just being myself. John's gospel of the washing of the feet came to mind as I played cribbage. I was deeply moved. I had come to serve, but they had ministered to me. We had indeed washed each other's feet. I left to prepare supper for my family truly filled with the Holy Spirit busting out of me."

There are so many people with gifts and so many needs. The Lord Jesus at his coming at Christmas invites us to just reach out and use them.

Evangelization

An evangelist is one who proclaims the good news—that God loves us, that Jesus is our Lord and Savior, lived, died and rose again in order to share his divine life with us. And through the power of the Holy Spirit we form one body, one people in Christ.

An evangelist is one whom God uses to bring another to an initial faith, to a conversion, or to a renewed faith in Christ. But we must not get the impression that the work of evangelization is reserved for a special group of people like for example, Rev. Billy Graham or a preacher at a parish mission. Handing on the faith is a responsibility of every member of the Church.

How did we first come to know God's love for us? How did we first become acquainted with Jesus who was born at Bethlehem, died on the cross for us, and rose from the dead? Was it not from our parents whose faith brought us in contact with an all-loving God? Yes, we first come to respond to the grace of God through our parents, our grandparents, our family and through the parish community.

The *General Catechetical Directory* says "Evangelization has its purpose to arouse the beginning of faith."

Catechesis follows this. Catechesis presupposes this initial faith and is concerned with nurturing it, strengthening it, making it active and mature. Some catechesis is given in a formal way in religious instruction classes and some comes in an informal way through the family, through reading Catholic papers, through participating in the liturgy and feasts of the Church year, through youth programs, participating in discussion groups, retreats, adult education classes, prayer meetings and in many other ways.

The whole Christian life is a continual process of conversion and growth, re-conversion and continual growth in faith through catechesis. An individual is likely at some point to be ready for another leap forward—a new experience of conversion which serves as a basis for more intense catechesis. We may go through periods of doubt, confusion, or dryness. And then through the witness of a fellow Christian we become open to the grace of God moving us to turn to him.

This was one of the central insights of the 1977 World Synod of Bishops. Namely, that conversion and continual growth in faith is a lifelong process and is at the very center of the Christian life. The Synod also pointed out that each one of us is called to share our faith, to be witnesses, evangelists and catechists. Pope Paul VI recently said, "We wish to confirm once more that the task of evangelizing all people constitutes the essential mission of the Church. The Church (that is, all of us) exists in order to evangelize."

Why is it then that we do it so poorly or so rarely? All of us have friends and close relatives who have fallen away from the practice of their faith. So many Catholic adults are inactive or do not participate any more. There are huge numbers of people that consider themselves Catholics, continue to attend church services and fulfill minimal duties of church membership but have never really been converted; for if they were once believers in the Lord Jesus and his teachings they have now forgotten that a follower of Christ is one who has turned his life over to him.

Every parish community needs programs of adult catechesis, Bible study and a continual study of the teachings of the Catholic faith. "Lord, I believe. Help my lack of trust." Every member of the Church needs to share his or her faith, talk about the joy of Christ's presence in his/her life. All of us need to share our faith with our children, with each other.

Jesus said, "Go therefore and make disciples of every nation. You will receive power when the Holy Spirit comes down upon you. Then you will be witnesses to the ends of the earth." Where are our Catholic witnesses? Where are the members of the Church that take seriously their call to invite others to share in the life of the Church?

A Bishop's Worries

Writing is one of the hardest things I do. I worry and fret over it...I pace the floor...I try to put it off...I get a cup of coffee...I look at the mail...I take a little nap to clear my mind...I do other things, first...

I try to think of what I should write about; something that can lift up and inspire; something that can remind you and me (Yes, I write for myself too) of what the Lord is calling us to be as his people.

I am pressed in by all kinds of concerns. I tend to be discouraged by the enormous task ahead. I struggle to keep up. I must have at least one hundred personal letters in my drawer waiting to be answered—people who have sent notes of encouragement or thanks, people asking for prayers and advice. Almost every week there is a request to speak in some part of the country. I have to turn most of them down, but I cannot ignore them all. I have responsibilities to the whole Church.

I participate in state, national and international meetings of bishops. This too is part of my calling. But the time and energy expended is enormous.

There are demands on all sides for my personal involvement. Come to this meeting—solve this problem—write this letter—celebrate with us—prepare a homily—write a chapter for a book—transcribe a few tapes.

My desk is loaded. Files are all around me. Reminder notes are scattered about. Piles of books, magazines and papers remain to be read or at least scanned.

I worry about the shortage of priests, about the appointment of priests to parishes and other diocesan offices. I'm especially concerned about those who are sick, discouraged, worn out and those who are thinking about leaving the active ministry. I see a bleak future with no young men in the major seminary and so few in college seminaries preparing for priesthood.

My soul cries out, "Lord, what do you want us to do?"

There are so many of us who have never really known a personal Lord who saved and redeemed us and who calls us to an intimate relationship with him.

I am discouraged about the many young people, so filled with idealism and hope, who have turned off any active participation in the life of the Church, who find their membership in the Church meaningless and who often critically point to the example or lack of example of adults around them.

"Lord," I cry, "What do you want us to do?"

I hear him say, "I am with you. I promised to send my Spirit. He will teach you all things. He will give you life and strength."

Then I look around and see the evidence of renewal in the Church. There is a shortage of ordained priests. But there is an enormous interest in ministries of all kinds. It is so encouraging to see active involvement of people in parish and diocesan councils, education, rural life and family life groups. It is a joy to realize that there is an army of dedicated women serving in countless ways in the life of parish communities. I rejoice at and encourage women to share fully in the ministries to which they are called by Christ.

I am continually impressed by the seriousness with which young people are prepared for the Sacrament of Confirmation. Parents, sponsors, grandparents, relatives and friends gather around the candidates as they eagerly declare their faith in the Lord Jesus and open themselves to life in the Spirit.

I could point to many other signs of renewal in parish life: preparation for and celebration of Baptism, first Confession and first Communion, Bible study groups, renewal of the Sacrament of Reconciliation, active preparation for marriage, Marriage Encounter, a growing interest in youth ministry, active involvement in the political process, support for our mission in Guatemala, the growing interest in prayer, prayer groups and Life in the Spirit seminars.

The Lord is good. It is a great time to be alive.

The mandate of Jesus is to bring the good news of life and salvation to all people. "You are to be my witnesses to the ends of the earth."

The ends of the earth are not "out there," but right here in our families, in our parishes, in our communities.

Puebla And Our Mission In Guatemala

Shortly after the announcement of my appointment as Bishop of the Diocese of New Ulm, I received word that our missionaries in San Lucas Toliman wanted to see me.

They wanted to tell me of the work of the mission. On their faces were signs of worry and concern. They were anxious about how the new bishop of New Ulm felt about our involvement in San Lucas. Would he continue to support and encourage the mission in Guatemala begun by Bishop Schladweiler and the people of the diocese some thirteen years before?

They presented me with a wall hanging beautifully embroidered by one of the women of the village with the plaintive plea, "Rev. Bishop, we beg God and you for your help for Project San Lucas." They gave me a delicately lettered scroll signed by hundreds of the villagers offering prayers and congratulations. Actually, most of the "signatures" were thumb prints of poor people who never had an opportunity to learn how to read and write.

They also gave me a magnificent ceramic dove and a hand woven stole which are masterful examples of the creativity and expert craftsmanship of these beautiful people.

I cried as I told them how proud I was of the work that they and the people of the diocese were dong in San Lucas. I was convinced then and I am even more convinced now that the mission is not a burden to us. It is a blessing. We established the mission with the intention of reaching out with loving care to a people oppressed with poverty and exploitation, weakened by sickness and malnutrition, and held back by a lack of education and opportunity.

In reality we have received much more than we have given. Our commitment to the mission has reminded us of our responsibility as followers of Jesus Christ to feed the hungry, to clothe the naked, to shelter the homeless. It has given us an opportunity to be personally concerned for a family without hope, to care for an orphan, to respond to the needs of people made homeless by a devastating earthquake, to help people move out of servitude to the pride of owning a bit of land, of practicing a trade, of learning how to read and write. It has given us an awareness of what poverty is like, the way so many people live in misery, and the injustices brought about when a small percentage of the people own all the land.

When Pope John Paul II went to Puebla, Mexico, to open the General Conference of Latin American Bishops, he spoke especially about evangelization, about Jesus the Son of God, about Mary the special patroness of the Latin American people, and about the mission of the Church.

He said, "As an evangelizer, Christ first of all proclaims a kingdom, the kingdom of God. As the kernal and center of his good news, Christ proclaims salvation from everything which oppresses man but which is above all liberation from sin and the evil one."

He said his strongest words when he spoke out forcefully in defense of human rights and when he invited Christians "to commit themselves to constructing a more just, humane and habitable world which does not close itself in, but rather, opens itself to God."

"It is not enough for the Christian to denounce injustices," he declared to the workers at Guadalajara, "he is asked to be a real witness and promoter of justice."

The Holy Father spelled out in detail what it means to make this world more just. "It means, among other things, to make the effort to strive to have a world in which no more children lack sufficient nutrition, education, instruction;...that there be no more poor peasants without land so that they can live and develop with dignity;...that there be no more who have too much while others are lacking everything through no fault of their own; that there not be so many families who are broken, disunited, insufficiently attended;...that force not prevail over truth and rights, but rather truth and rights over force; and that the economic and political never prevail over the human.

"But do not be content with a more human world. Make an explicitly more divine world, more according to God, governed by faith and that which faith inspires—the moral, religious and social progress of man."

Now these are the things that our mission in Guatemala is trying to accomplish with its educational, doctrinal and socio-economic programs. And the people of the diocese have responded with their help and support.

One day last fall a local farmer came in with a check for three thousand dollars. Three months later he brought in another check for the same amount. The check represented a percentage of a bountiful harvest of corn and soybeans. The Lord had blessed him, and he was turning part of it back to the Lord. He knew that the money would go to the poor people without subtracting any administrative costs. He said, "I want to give money where I know that people who receive it are making their lives better. I have seen how hard these people work."

Another man gets up at 5:30 every morning and spends the first hours of every day writing personal reminders and thank you notes to hundreds of people all over the United States. Through his efforts eight thousand dollars a year is given to the mission.

There are groups of people who meet regularly to sew for the mission, who produce things to sell for the benefit of the people of San Lucas, who sponsor orphans, who support farmers while they terrace mountain land and who do all kinds of creative things to raise money for the mission school, the orphanage, the clinic and other parish programs.

Hundreds of people have gone to Guatemala at their own expense to see the work of the mission first hand and have returned appalled at the poverty and more determined to do their part to respond to the needs of people in the third world.

There is a parish in the diocese which gives ten per cent of its total income to the poor of the United States and the world. One half of that is given to the mission.

Another parish urged each family to contribute two bushels of corn. The grain was sold for a thousand dollars which was sent to San Lucas.

I have been to San Lucas several times, I witnessed the gentle ways and the strong faith of the people. I observed the regular meetings of hundreds of catechists as they sang and prayed and studied to be better witnesses of the good news of salvation. I saw the joy on the faces of children who attended the school and who are lovingly cared for in the orphanage. I was amazed at the long lines of the sick and injured who come to the clinic each day. And I observed the signs of hope as men reclaimed land, learned trades, built homes and found jobs.

It had been the hope and plan of the mission staff to be able to turn over the socio-economic program completely to the people by 1980. They are ready now. With a low interest loan from the diocese some fourteen projects including land development, animal raising, food production, carpentry, and stone masonry have a small capital fund to work with and are on their own.

Renewal Of The Church

I am greatly encouraged by the growing number of people who take an active part in the life of their parishes, engaging in various ministries of the word, of worship and of service. They are responding to gifts that the Holy Spirit gives them. I meet them at confirmations, parish celebrations and diocesan meetings of all kinds. They teach religion, lead youth groups, direct music groups, clean and decorate the church, lead prayer groups, read the scripture passages at Mass, serve at the altar, distribute Holy Communion, visit the sick, comfort the elderly, promote the cause of justice and in so many other ways build up the Body of Christ.

But there are so many *other* people out there, God's people, who as members of the Body of Christ are his hands and feet, mouth and heart in our society. I wonder if what I write has any meaning for them. I have a feeling that a large majority of us think and speak and act as though all of this talk about the people of God, participation in the life of the Church, using the gifts of the Holy Spirit to minister to others—all of this is for priests, religious, parish ministers and the few others in the parish who have volunteered to work with them.

If this is our view, then we have missed a major point in the renewal of the Church that the Vatican Council called us to.

When we speak of the role of the laity in the Church we have to continually emphasize that every member of the Church has a unique ministry to bring Jesus and his message to the world in which we live. Somehow, the Word of God has to come alive in that world. It is the vocation of lay people to do God's work in the context of their ordinary positions in the world. No one else can take their place.

I speak to each one of you and say that you should see your role as one who serves others in the name of Christ Jesus. There is a Christian significance to your ordinary, daily life as lay people in the world.

To cite just a couple of examples. Parents, in your daily live and concern for your children, in your countless sacrifices and devotion to one another, in your fidelity, you are a sign of the love and sacrifice of Jesus for his people.

Those of you in the health care field, every day you serve people as healers. You hold out the loving, healing hand of Christ to suffering and hurting people.

Those of you in local and state government, you represent people and their needs. You are by definition servants of people to build a better society in which to live.

Business people of all kinds provide services to others. I could go on.

What I am trying to say is that as God's people you should see that only you can bring Christ and his message to a world that has so often forgotten Him. Somehow the message of love, of justice, of kindness, of forgiveness, of fidelity, of holiness has to be brought to life in that world.

I will continue to call people to special ministries within the Church. In doing that I do not mean to forget God's work is carried out in many ways through the worldly vocation of a family man, of a mother, of a therapist or typist.

Jesus said, "Bring the message of the Gospel to the whole world."

Lent—A Call To Conversion

Lent is one of my favorite times of the year. Although it is a hard time, a penitential time, it is so filled with hope and the promise of good things. Lent is death before the new life, darkness before the light, quiet before the glorious alleluia.

Lent conjures up in my mind many images of the past and present: forty days of Jesus in the desert, having only one full meal a day, purple vestments, no drinking, stations of the cross, the coming of spring, house cleaning, putting aside something for Rice Bowl, daily Mass, giving to the hungry of the world, lenten devotions, family prayer, no cigarettes, helping others.

Yes, Lent is a call to penance. Lord knows we need it. We are so easily persuaded to satisfy all our desires, to possess all that we want. With voluntary penance we say no. We freely give up some things, not because they are bad in themselves, but to give us strength to say no to those things and those relationships that keep us from the Lord.

As a bare minimum we are obliged as Catholics to abstain from meat on Ash Wednesday and on the Fridays of Lent. Most of us are obliged to fast, that is to eat only one full meal, on Ash Wednesday and Good Friday.

We are all invited, encouraged to do much more. Many of us try to fast every day during Lent. Others try to eat nothing between meals. Still others quit smoking or abstain from alcoholic drink. One of the best penances is to give to the poor. Our mission in Guatemala is a constant reminder of the starving, the needy, and those unjustly oppressed.

It is necessary for every Christian to do penance. "Unless you do penance, you will perish," the Lord said. "Whomever wishes to be my follower must deny his very self, take up his cross each day, and follow in my steps." (Lk. 9:23)

Lent is a call to conversion. Conversion is a life-long process: turning to the Lord in faith and turning away from sin. "This is the time of fulfillment. The reign of God is at hand! Reform your lives and believe in the gospel." (Mk 1:14)

Those are the words we hear as we come to receive the ashes on the first day of Lent. "Reform your life. Believe in the good news." We bow our heads and quietly say, "Yes, Lord, I will."

Lent means to walk with Jesus on his journey to Jerusalem. "We must now go up to Jerusalem. The Son of Man will be delivered up to the Gentiles. He will be mocked and outraged and spat upon. They will scourge him and put him to death, and on the third day he will rise again." (Lk. 18:31-33)

The passion, death and resurrection is the center of our faith in Jesus. We have been immersed in that mystery at our baptism. We renew it each time we celebrate the Holy Eucharist. I believe that in recent years greater numbers of people have really tried to participate in daily Mass during Lent.

I can think of no better way to enter into the spirit of the season than by receiving the sacraments and meditating on the daily scripture readings.

The Language Of The Church

I would like to share with you a list of definitions or descriptions of terms that are in widespread use these days, but frequently are misunderstood.

Church—In the language of the Second Vatican Council, the Church is a mystery, a communion, the assembly of all those who believe in Christ, the kingdom of Christ now present in mystery, the Body of Christ, the People of God.

All of us together (bishops, priests, religious and laity) are the Church. It is a great mystery that we form one Body, one people, with Jesus as the head and center and the Holy Spirit as the life and power. We are a pilgrim people, sinful and weak, yet armed with the grace and gifts of the Holy Spirit to do great things in a world which so easily forgets God's great love for us.

The Church is also an institution with leadership, authority and structure.

Mission of the Church—A mission statement is a statement of purpose. The Church has no other purpose for its existence than to extend the kingdom of God to people of every nation, of every age, of every social and economic condition. The mission of the Church in the Diocese of New Ulm must be the same as the mission of Jesus.

Local Church—The local Church is the diocese, that portion of God's people, living in one territory, which is entrusted to a bishop to be shepherded by him with the cooperation of the presbytery. As a local Church the bishop, priests, religious and laity of the diocese from one people. We are bound together as a communion (community) of one faith, one divine life, one call to love, celebrating the same sacraments with Jesus as our center and the Holy Spirit as our source of life and power. We are united with the other local Churches throughout the world in proclaiming our Holy Father, Pope John Paul II, as the visible head of the universal Church.

Bishop—The bishop is the leader, the shepherd of the local Church. The bishop is the visible principle and foundation of unity in the local Church. He is also the link between the local Church and the universal Church.

The bishop's role is to teach the word of God, to preside over Christian worship, to gather together and oversee the diocese, to choose and direct helpers in the ministry and to discern the special gifts that the Spirit gives his people.

Presbytery—All priests, by their ordination, are bound together in an intimate sacramental brotherhood. "In a special way they form one presbytery in a diocese to whose service they are committed under their own bishop." (Vat. II, Priests, 8)

United among themselves and with the bishop of the diocese, the welfare of the whole diocese is their concern. They are ready to serve the people of the diocese wherever their gifts and talents can be used best in the local Church.

Council of Priests—The Council of Priests is the "assembly or senate of priests, representing the presbytery, which can with its advice assist the bishop effectively in the government of the diocese." (Vat. II, Priests, 7) It must be established in every diocese.

"Through this council the priests recognize that they are mutually complementary in serving one and the same mission of the Church." (Directory for Bishops) "Through the council the bishop hears the views of his priests and discusses with them the pastoral needs and the good of the diocese." (Directory for Bishops)

Sisters' Council—The Sisters' Council represents all of the sisters serving in a diocese. It is established to foster the spiritual, professional and cultural enrichment of sisters; to ensure adequate involvement of the sisters in policy-making decisions on diocesan, regional and parish levels; to encourage sisters to minister; to work with groups to foster justice and peace; to serve as a channel of communication among sisters and the bishop and other councils and organizations and to foster religious vocations.

Diocesan Pastoral Council—The Diocesan Pastoral Council is a body representing the people of the diocese, priests, religious and laity. It is set up to investigate and carefully consider whatever pertains to diocesan pastoral activities, weigh them carefully, and arrive at practical conclusions to help the people of God pattern their lives and actions more closely on the Gospel. By its study and reflection, the council furnishes the judgements necessary to enable the diocesan community to plan its pastoral program systematically and to fulfill it effectively. The Council has a consultative voice; nevertheless, the bishop has great respect for its recommendations, for it offers him the serious and settled cooperation of the diocesan community.

To make the council's work more effective, it is necessary that parish councils be set up and aligned with the diocesan council through the regional councils. The Diocesan Pastoral Council is especially concerned with recommending goals for the local church. Committees of the DPC, especially evangelization and catechesis, worship and spiritual renewal, administration and personnel are responsible for setting objectives. Objectives outline steps that will be taken each year to reach the goals.

Parish—The diocese is divided into a number of parish communities, each with histories, traditions, family bonds, economic and social relationships. They are communities of faith-filled, worshipping, caring people. The mission (purpose) of each parish is the same as the mission of the diocese and the mission of Jesus. Jesus calls each member of the Church to take an active part in his mission. It is primarily in the parish community that all of this happens. That is where God's people live and work. They have to say to themselves, "What would Jesus do? What does Jesus want us to be and to do in our community?"

As a parish community we are to hand on the faith to children and youth and adults, to those who have dropped out, to those who are searching. We are to worship the Father and build up fellowship in the life of the spirit through the Mass and the sacraments, through prayer and penance. We are to reach out in loving service to others, to the poor and the sick, to the elderly and the lonely, to people in mission countries. We are to work for justice in our society. If any of these is missing, the mission of the Church is not being accomplished.

Ministry—Ministry means service. It means to serve others in the name of Jesus Christ. A minister is one who attends to the needs of others. Ministries flow from the gifts of the Spirit. The Holy Spirit gives many gifts for the building up of God's people, whether within the Church or in the broader human community.

Evangelization—Evangelization has as its purpose to arouse the beginnings of faith. Every member of the Church has a part in sharing the faith and in leading others, children and youth and especially adults, to a personal commitment to Jesus Christ and his Church. Pope Paul VI said that "the task of evangelizing all people constitutes the essential mission of the Church. The Church exists in order to evangelize."

Catechesis—Catechesis is intended to make one's faith become living, conscious and active, through the light of instruction. Catechesis means every act of the Church which aims at developing and deepening faith. It includes formal programs of religious education in Catholic schools and in the Confraternity of Christian Doctrine. It also, and even more importantly, means the sharing of faith that takes place in the family, the parish and the community.

Theology—Theology is concerned with faith seeking understanding. It is the systematic and scientific investigation of the truths of faith.

Liturgy—Liturgy is the public worship of the Church, including the Sacrifice of the Mass, the celebration of the sacraments, the liturgical year, and the divine office. The Vatican Council declared that "the liturgy is the summit toward which the activity of the Church is directed; at the same time it is the fountain from which all her power flows." "In the restoration and promotion of the sacred liturgy, full and active participation by all the people is the aim to be considered before all else." Servers, lectors, commentators, musicians, communion distributors, members of liturgy committees, exercise a genuine liturgical ministry.

Charismatic Renewal—Every member of the Church is given gifts or charisms. In that sense every Christian is a charismatic or one gifted by God. The charismatic renewal calls people to a more explicit and active acceptance of gifts of the Holy Spirit.

Social Concerns—This is the title given to a broad range of ministries in which people attend to the needs of others and work for justice and peace in our society. The Lord Jesus gave us the example of seeking out the sick, the crippled, the blind and the deaf, the poor and the oppressed. He ministered to them, comforted them, helped them. Each member of the Christian community is called to do the same.

Stewardship—A steward is one who manages the property, the money or the affairs of another. Christian stewardship recognizes that everything that we have, money, land, property, talents and life itself are gifts of God. We are not absolute masters of them; we have to give an account of our stewardship. Total stewardship deals with the right use and management of all of God's gifts of time, talent and treasure.

Pastoral—Pastor is a Latin word meaning shepherd. Jesus is the Good Shepherd who knows his sheep, cares for them, feeds them and offers his life for them. "I myself will pasture my sheep; I myself will give them rest, says the Lord God. The lost I will seek out, the strayed I will bring back, the injured I will bind up, the sick I will heal, shepherding them rightly." (Ez 34:15-16)

A Christian pastor is charged with the spiritual care of people. Pastoral councils and pastoral offices are likewise concerned with all of those things that build up God's people: strengthening the community, handing on and fostering growth in faith, good teaching, active participation in the worship and praise of God, fostering prayer and spiritual growth, supporting family life, reaching out to the sick, the needy and the oppressed, working for justice and peace.

Christmas Celebrates Love

Christmas is a time for love. It celebrates love. It remembers love.

Think of the many images of Christmas time: Jesus in the manger, Mary, the message of the angels, shepherds, the wise men, gifts, lights, carols, joy. They all tell of God's ever faithful and merciful love toward every single human being. And they all challenge us to love God unconditionally and to love one another as He loved us.

Pope John Paul II wrote an encyclical called *Rich in Mercy*, about the ever faithful, loving mercy of God. It is one of the central mysteries of our faith. God's mercy—a reality so rich in meaning that it is difficult to express in words that are adequate.

The Bible says: "God is rich in mercy; because of His great love for us He brought us to life with Christ when we were dead to sin." (Eph 2:4-5) "The Lord God is merciful and gracious, slow to anger, abounding in steadfast love and faithfulness." (Ex. 34:6)

It is unfortunate that there is no single word in our language that conveys the riches of the biblical concept. The words that we translate as "mercy" mean steadfast, enduring, everlasting love. They mean kindness, tender, unmerited, faithful love. The meaning that we most often give to the English word "mercy" is to show pity, to spare. It only rarely means this in the Bible.

No wonder that when the Pope writes a major encyclical on the loving mercy of God we fail to catch the excitement. We think it strange that he chose this topic for a letter to the Christian people. We just do not grasp what he is talking about.

Yet is not the mystery of the Father's love and mercy toward us at the very center of Jesus' teaching? God loves us. He calls us to be his very own people, his family, his spouse. he sent his only begotten Son to show his merciful love. The beloved disciple wrote, "See what love the Father has bestowed on us in letting us be called Children of God!" (I Jn 3:1) He goes on, "God's love was revealed in our midst in this way: He sent his only Son to the world that we might have life through him. Love, then, consists in this: not that we have loved God, but that he has loved us and has sent his Son as an offering for our sins." (I Jn 4:9-10)

One of the great experiences of my life was when I really came to know that God loves me. Oh, I knew that God loved me in a general sort of way. But there was a day when it took on a new meaning. Imagine, God the Creator and Lord of all, the One who is and was, loves *me*. He chose me. He holds me in his hands. He sent his son for *me*. "Can a mother forget her infant? Even should she forget, I will never forget you." (Is 49:15)

How he loves us! With an everlasting love, a merciful love that is faithful and never changes even though we forget him, even if we reject him, even if we sin against him.

People tell me that one of the greatest days of their lives was the one on which they realized, really realized that God loved them.

Why do so many people have so much difficulty believing in the loving mercy of God? We all feel so inadequate, so inferior. "How can God love me?" we say. I am no good. I have been so bad. You name it, I have done it." Young people, especially, so often have a poor image of themselves.

Yet the good news that Jesus came to bring us is just that: God loves me. He doesn't love me only when I am good or because I am good. He just loves me. He made me. He continues to care for me. He sent his Son to prove it. Even when I sin? Yes!

That is what the encyclical is all about: the loving mercy of God, the merciful love of God. Jesus revealed God "above all in his relationship of love for man." And this love "becomes visible in Christ and through Christ through his actions and his words, and finally through his death on the Cross and his Resurrection."

Jesus not only speaks of the merciful love of God, "above all he makes it incarnate and personifies it. He himself is mercy." Through Christ, God becomes visible as the Father who is "rich in mercy."

When the messengers of John the Baptist came to Jesus to ask him: "Are you the one who is to come, or shall we look for another?" (Lk 7:19) Jesus told them that the Messiah would be known by his loving kindness toward others: "Go and tell John what it is that you have seen and heard: the blind receive their sight, the lame walk, lepers are cleansed, and the deaf hear, the dead are raised up, the poor have good news preached to them." (Lk. 7:22-23)

The merciful love of God "is able to reach down to every prodigal son or daughter, to every human misery, and above all to every form of moral misery, to sin." The Cross of Christ speaks to us as a sign of the eternal love of God for each member of the human race. For God "so loved the world, that he gave his only son, that whosoever believes in him should not perish but have eternal life." (Jn 3:16) This love is more powerful than any kind of evil, even death.

The Holy Father's message to us is that as followers of Christ we are called to the same mission as Jesus was. In our lives we are to bear witness to God's mercy. We are to work for justice, for "justice is based on love, flows from it and tends toward it."

You may have read about Dorothy Day who died a few years ago. She challenged all of us to love God unconditionally and to love one another as he loved us. She believed in voluntary poverty, and practiced direct action for the poor. She so beautifully saw the connection between merciful love and working for justice.

At Christmas time our Holy Father reminds us that side by side with people living in plenty and ruled by consumerism and pleasure, the same human family contains individuals and groups that are living in want, suffering, misery and often actually dying of hunger.

Pope John Paul II has a powerful message for us: God in his merciful love has given us everything. We need to love in return. May the tender mercy of God be with you at this holy season and always.

Mary, The Mother Of God

In 1981, I received a letter from Pope John Paul II inviting me, or at least some of the bishops from each conference, to come to Rome on the Feast of Pentecost to celebrate the anniversaries of the Councils of Constantinople and Ephesus.

These are not ordinary anniversaries. The Council of Constantinople was the second Ecumenical Council of the Church held in the year 381. This is the sixteenth centenary of that event. This year is also the 1550th anniversary of the Council of Ephesus held in 431. The Church has a long memory.

These fourth and fifth century Councils were significant milestones in the history of the Church. In those early days great controversies arose over the central truths of our faith in the Blessed Trinity and in Jesus Christ, true God and true man.

From the Council of Constantinople (and Nicea held in 325) we get the Creed that we recite each Sunday at Mass expressing faith in the fullness of the Blessed Trinity: Father, Son and Holy Spirit. A particular heritage of that Council is the doctrine on the Holy Spirit whom we proclaim as "Lord, the giver of life, who proceeds from the Father and the Son. With the Father and the Son he is worshipped and glorified."

The Council of Ephesus defined the two natures, the divine and the human, in the one person Jesus Christ who is our Lord and Savior. As that Council was beginning the people acclaimed Mary with the title "Mother of God." And this was the touchstone of the true Catholic faith. Mary is not only the mother of the man, Jesus. She is the mother of Jesus, the second person of the Blessed Trinity who is both God and fully human.

So the celebration in Rome in an important one. What could be more important than these central mysteries of our faith which were so clearly defined in those early years. The Holy Father wrote: "These two anniversaries, though for different reasons and with differing historical relevance, redound to the honor of the Holy Spirit. All was accomplished *by the power of the Holy Spirit.* One can see how profoundly these two commemorations, to which it is proper to make reference in this year of the Lord 1981, are linked to one another in the teaching and in the profession of faith of the Church, of the faith of all Christians. Faith in the Most Holy Trinity: Faith in the Father, from whom all gifts come. Faith in Christ the Redeemer of the human race. Faith in the Holy Spirit. And, in this light, veneration of the Blessed Virgin, who by thus consenting to the divine utterance...became the Mother of Jesus."

Mary is such a good example for us. She was not used by God in merely a passive way. She "cooperated in the work of human salvation through free faith and obedience." (Vatican II, *The Church*, n. 56)

Mary is the Mother of the Church and was closely united with the work of the Holy Spirit at the incarnation and birth of our Savior and at the birth of the Church in the Upper Room at Pentecost.

Our life in the Spirit, our relationship with the Lord needs constant renewal and growth. We are so weak and need to cry out, "Come Holy Spirit, fill the hearts of your faithful and renew the face of the earth."

So many of the questions and problems of today are concerned with life. Human life, human rights and dignity are trampled by selfishness, greed, lust and injustice.

Abortion is an abominable crime, an attack on human life at its most vulnerable moment. This cries out for a change of heart.

Millions are deprived of the most elementary human rights and are forced to live in poverty and starvation. We see that in our own mission in Guatemala. This too cries out for a change of heart.

All recent popes have condemned the arms race. We cannot continue as a nation to lead the world in the manufacture and sale of weapons. Again it is a life issue and cries out for a change of heart.

The use of nuclear weapons against population centers is immoral. Nor can the threat to use them in such a way be justified. It cries out for a change of heart.

The renewal of God's people called for and initiated by the Second Vatican Council can be carried out only in the Holy Spirit. Renewal begins first and foremost within people's souls since no renewal is possible without continual conversion to God.

I have experienced the power of the Holy Spirit in my own life. My faith in recent years has become deeper, more personal. Jesus has become real, a close friend to whom I can speak and listen. I have become more aware of the gifts that the Spirit gives and how he uses me in unexpected and unplanned ways.

Liturgical Renewal

Since the revision of the rite for Confirmation, preparation for the sacrament has enormously improved. One- to three-year programs are common. Special retreats, service projects, parental involvement, letters to the Bishop are all part of an effort to help young people to respond in faith to the call of the Lord as adult, responsible members of the Church.

One of the significant changes has been the gradual advance of the age of confirmation from sixth, seventh and eighth grade to ninth, tenth or eleventh grade. The older ones are so much better able to understand their responsibilities, to commit themselves to the Lord Jesus and his teachings.

Celebrating the liturgy in so many parishes gives me an opportunity to observe the progress that is being made to improve the quality of liturgical worship. Often when I come home late at night, some member of the diocesan staff asks me, "How did it go tonight?" Usually I say, "It was really good." Sometimes, "Excellent." Other times I have to say, "It was just okay."

What makes the difference? One can detect a certain spirit, a quality of reverence and evident faith, and the degree of participation on the part of those who attend.

In a key passage of the *Constitution on the Sacred Liturgy,* the Second Vatican Council declares, "Mother Church earnestly desires that all the faithful be led to that full, conscious and active participation in liturgical celebrations which is demanded by the very nature of the liturgy. Such participation by the Christian people as 'a chosen race, a royal priesthood, a holy nation, a purchased people' (I Pet. 2:9) is their right and duty by reason of their baptism."

"In the restoration and promotion of the sacred liturgy," the document continues, "this full and active participation is the aim to be considered before all else; for it is the primary and indispensable source from which the faithful are to derive the true Christian spirit. Therefore, through the needed program of instruction, pastors of souls must zealously strive to achieve it in all their pastoral work." (n. 14)

"Active and full participation." This comes from a faith and reverence from the depth of our being as we recognize that we join with Jesus, the one high priest and mediator, in giving worship and praise to God in those sacred mysteries. It comes from an appreciation of the great privilege that is ours to participate in mind, body and heart through our actions and bodily attitudes, our attention and listening, our singing, responses and acclamations and also at times by our reverent silence. The *Constitution on the Liturgy* reminds us that each one of us has a proper role in the liturgy and no one can be a passive spectator. "In liturgical celebrations, whether as a minister or as one of the faithful, each person should perform his/her role by doing solely and totally what the nature of things and liturgical norms require of him/her. Servers, lectors, commentators and members of the choir also exercise a genuine liturgical ministry." (n. 28-29)

What a joy it is to participate in a parish liturgy where everyone joins in the singing, where there is faith-filled attention, where the readings are proclaimed with understanding, where there is an enthusiastic response to the prayers, where there is deep faith in the presence of the Lord Jesus and in the reception of Holy Communion. Such a situation does not happen easily nor without planning, preparation and instruction.

For "full, conscious and active participation" the Word of God must be proclaimed distinctly, intelligently, slowly and with conviction. In many parishes this is done well. In others much more needs to be done. For example, the Word of God must never be proclaimed from a missalette or a sheet of paper. Lectors need to learn how to use the Lectionary. We need adequate sound systems and even more instruction on how to properly speak through them. Ordinarily, lectors should be adults. Children should proclaim the Word of God in the main parish liturgy only when they are especially well prepared.

At a recent Confirmation two young people read the scriptures with such meaning that the whole congregation was spellbound. It was a delight. It was also exceptional.

The choir has as its particular task to facilitate the participation of the congregation, sometimes through listening and reflection, but mostly through singing together. The Vatican II document says, "Whenever the sacred action is to be celebrated with song, the whole body of the faithful may be able to contribute that active participation which is rightly theirs." (n. 114)

It is so important, therefore, to have a leader of song who will direct the people, announce the proper place in the hymnal and practice with them when necessary.

Those who have been appointed as special distributors of the Holy Eucharist or who bring Holy Communion to the sick have a great responsibility to exercise this ministry with reverence and love and in accordance with the norms of the Church.

There is evidence of so much progress in liturgical renewal. I pray for an ever deepening participation of every member of the Church.

The Martyrs Of Latin America

I was deeply moved—yes, even shaken—by the death of Fr. Stanley Rother who was murdered by three assassins in his rectory at Santiago Atitlan, Guatemala. He was a hardworking, dedicated priest who gave his life in serving the impoverished and oppressed people of his village.

Along with hundreds of other bishops, priests, sisters, lay missionaries, catechists and other leaders in Latin America, he was put to death in the service of the Gospel. The bishops of Guatemala, speaking of the murder of nine other priests and numerous catechists, declared "These acts of violence cannot be isolated acts or casual events, but rather...a very carefully studied plan exists to intimidate the Church and silence its prophetic voice."

Father Stan was regarded with so much love and affection that he was made one of the elders of the community. Naturally, the people wanted him to be buried in Santiago. They understood, however, the wishes of his own family that he be buried in Oklahoma. In the sanctuary of the Church in Santiago the people buried his heart, other vital organs and the cloths with which they soaked up his blood.

I used to think that the age of martyrs was over. But there are martyrs in every period of Church history. A martyr is one who dies for his or her faith. The word martyr means a witness. Martyrs take a stand. They show by their lives what they believe. There are people all over the world who are willing to undergo prison, torture and death in following Christ. Christians in Lithuania and other countries behind the Iron Curtain continue to be systematically persecuted. All over Latin America Christians are being murdered precisely because they have taken an option for the poor and have recognized that working for justice is a constitutive part of the Christian message. Their dying is in imitation of the death of Christ.

On the feast of a martyr, we read this Gospel passage: "Unless a grain of wheat falls to the earth and dies, it remains just a grain of wheat. But if it dies it produces much fruit." (John 12,24) This same text was used at the wake of Father Rother. At services in Guatemala City, Bishop Eduardo Fuentes called the priest a martyr, "for he came back to the parish in spite of threats to his life out of love and service to these people."

Father Stan had received a death threat and left the country. He returned a few months later, believing that the threat had subsided. Only a few days before his tragic death, at the annual fiesta in honor of St. James, patron of the town, Father Stan and neighboring priests witnessed a hundred marriages, baptized two or three hundred children and ministered to hundreds of other people who came to the fiesta. The martyrs of Latin America today remind us of our responsibility to witness to our own faith in our families and communities. I believe that underlying much of the persecution of the Church in Latin America is greed for money and power. We have to come to see that so many of us are affected by a greed for material things, somehow thinking that in them we will find our satisfaction and happiness.

Father Stan's death reminds us also of the need for continual support for our brothers and sisters in Guatemala. Because of the violence in that country, there are even more orphans, widows and starving people crying out for help.

As we pray for the repose of the soul of Fr. Stanley Rother, let us also pray for peace and justice in that country.

Nuclear Weapons

I want to talk to you just as clearly as I can about issues of the greatest importance in our day: war, the arms race and nuclear weapons. I have thought and prayed about these issues for a long time. I have read addresses and encyclicals of recent popes and documents of the Vatican Council, writings of other bishops and theologians and Sacred Scripture itself.

I will present my ideas in a series of short sentences. I want to be sure that my position is clear, even though a great deal needs to be said on the subject.

1. *War is evil.* On this there can be no doubt. War brings nothing but human misery, suffering and grief. We all recall the ringing words of Pope Paul VI, who went in 1965 to the United Nations to appeal for an end of all wars. He cried, "No more war. War never again!" Soon after, he established January 1 as a day to be celebrated each year for peace.

Pope John Paul II, speaking at his residence in Castel Gandolfo, declared "War is destruction of human life. War is death." Speaking at Hiroshima last February, John Paul II said, "Let us make a solemn decision, now, that war will never be tolerated and seen as a means for resolving differences."

2. *The use of nuclear weapons even in a "just" war is evil.* For many centuries theologians have taught that it is possible to have a just war. Such a war may be fought only in defense or as a means of restoring violated rights. It can be engaged in only as a last resort and with a reasonable chance for victory. The good to be achieved must outweigh the evil that must result from the war. There is another condition which must be present before a war can be considered just. The means used in conducting the war must be just. Innocent civilians must be protected. Obliteration bombing or the destruction of whole cities must be condemned.

69

Therefore, even in a so-called just war the use of nuclear bombing is immoral. There is no question that nuclear warheads may not be used in offense. In a defensive war, there is no way that the use of nuclear warheads can be justified because of their potential for massive destruction.

The Vatican Council declared, "Any act of war aimed indiscriminately at the destruction of entire cities or of extensive areas along with their population is a crime against God and man himself. It merits unequivocal and unhesitating condemnation."

There are some who would argue for the use of relatively small nuclear warheads in tactical situations. It is folly to think that once one side used even a small nuclear weapon that the other side would not retaliate to escalate the conflict into massive retaliation. It is my judgment that any use of nuclear weapons against an enemy is to be condemned.

3. *The threat to use atomic weapons is immoral.* In our statement of 1976, *To Live in Christ Jesus,* The American Catholic Bishops said, "As possessors of a vast nuclear arsenal, we must not attack civilian populations, and it is also wrong to threaten to attack them as a part of a strategy of deterrence. In other words, if there is no way that nuclear weapons can be used even for defensive purposes, the threat to use them can in no way be justified in Catholic moral teaching."

4. *It is immoral to possess nuclear weapons.* Nuclear weapons may not be used for attack or for a first strike. They may not be used in defense. Threatening to use nuclear weapons is wrong. Therefore, it seems to me that even to possess them is wrong.

The possibility of nuclear war is such an overpowering issue that all of us really need to work for disarmament. The arms race cannot go on. It is madness and folly. Preparations for war must be changed into working for justice and peace. This calls for a conversion of heart. "The arms race," the Vatican Council said, "is an utterly treacherous trap for humanity and one that injures the poor to an intolerable degree."

Jesus is the Prince of Peace. His victory over sin and death, his promised gift of endless life came through his suffering, death and resurrection. By the Holy Cross he redeemed the world. He invites us to follow him not only to the glory of the resurrection, but first to the cross. "If a man wishes to come after me, he must deny his very self, take up his cross and follow in my steps. Whoever would preserve his life will lose it, but whoever loses his life for my sake and the Gospel's will preserve it." (Mark 8:34-35)

Those who work for peace must be also ready to accept persecution. Jesus said "Blessed are the peacemakers. They shall be called children of God." But he added "Blessed are those who are persecuted in the cause of right. Theirs is the Kingdom of Heaven." (Matt. 5:9-10)

All of us must pray for peace. We need to come to a real change in our attitudes toward solving conflicts. We need to be educated on the grave danger of nuclear armament and give public witness to this. We must be prepared to live without nuclear weapons and work to stop the arms race. I pray that the Lord will give us the time.

Spiritual Reflections

Lord, you have gifted me. You love me, just love me. Not for what I do, but as I am. You loved me from the beginning, holding me in your loving embrace. With an everlasting love, with faithful love. Lord you loved me first. You sent your son, Jesus, born of Mary, as the embodiment of your love. Thank you Lord.

Jesus took on our humanity, like us in all things except sin. He cried, laughed, suffered, was hungry, thirsty, tired. He felt abandoned, rejected. He was mocked, laughed at, criticized, tortured, put to death.

In all, he did his Father's will. He inaugurated his reign. The Father's reign was first in his own heart and body. "The kingdom of God is at hand." The kingdom is where God's will is done, wherever he is present.

Jesus wants to establish his kingdom in everyone. "All nations shall see the saving power of God," all peoples, of every nation, class, sex, race, of every social and economic condition. In every aspect of our life, God wants to reign, first in our minds and hearts, then in our bodies and actions. "The reign of God is within you."

Dear Father, you want to reign in my heart and mind and body. For this I just have to let you in. "May your kingdom come, may your will be done." You call me to continual conversion, change of heart, change of mind. Yes Lord, I believe in you. You are my Lord and Savior. Reign over me. Let there be in me your rule of truth, unselfish giving, kindness, reaching out, singleness of purpose, justice and peace.

The Lord uses me as I am. In this fragile vessel, sinful, broken, in constant need of healing, he gives me gifts. He has given me many. Praise Him. He wants me to use them to serve others in his name. This ministry is his work, it is his power. I am weak, and in need. It is OK. He knows that. I am a sinner and don't have it all together. He knows that. He calls me to repentance and forgiveness. "Lord I do believe; help my lack of trust."

Lord, don't let me allow the pressures on my time keep me from loving and ministering. I am a compulsive worker. "My work" becomes an obsession. I am preoccupied with my desk, endless reports, mountains of mail. Lord Jesus, don't let that keep me from going out to the people, those who I am especially called to shepherd.

I was praying one night in the half-darkened chapel. It was a good prayer. I felt a loving embrace from the Lord, as though he were standing behind me with his arms wrapped around me. Suddenly this insight, or this prayer came, "Lord, help me to admit my weakness." This prayer was so powerful, a real gift.

Lord Jesus, help me to admit my weakness. Help me to accept my humanness. You took on our human nature. You redeemed us in your humanity. You are our high priest precisely in that you became one of us in all things except sin. I love you Jesus. Help me to remember that this is your Church. You are the Head. You are the Lord. We are just your instruments, your fragile and broken vessels of clay.

"The favors of the Lord are not exhausted. His mercies are not spent." (Lam. 3,22)

Moral Issues

You have undoubtedly noticed that bishops, priests, sisters and laity all over the country have taken outspoken stands on public moral issues. A large amount of coverage has been given to this in the press, radio and television.

Reporters have asked me, "Why the sudden change? Why have church leaders taken positions contrary to U.S. Government policy?" Others have accused church leaders of mixing religion with politics.

A wide range of public controversies have been addressed by bishops either through official statements of the National Conference of Catholic Bishops, or through individual teaching in sermons, addresses, pastoral letters and newspaper articles. I have joined my fellow bishops in this.

We have declared immoral the use and the threat to use nuclear weapons. We have spoken out against the arms race and called for a nuclear weapons freeze by the United States and the Soviet Union. We have expressed concern for justice and peace in Central America and have opposed military aid for El Salvador. We have condemned abortion as an unspeakable abomination and have committed ourselves to support the Hatch Amendment. We have taken a consistent pro-life and pro-human rights stand on a variety of issues. We have spoken for fidelity, permanence and mutual love in marriage and defended it against a selfish and contraceptive mentality.

While less often mentioned in the media, bishops have spoken for racial equality, Christian feminism, the rights of farm workers, collective bargaining, stewardship of land and justice for farmers, gun control, reform of the penal system, rights for workers to organize and be represented by a union of their own choosing, and a host of other topics including a carefully reasoned statement against Marxism.

To say that church leaders are doing something new when they speak out on public issues in not true. The American bishops, since they began meeting together at the Baltimore Councils of the last century, have exercised their role as teachers, not only on matters of Church doctrine and discipline, but also on public issues of the day.

What is different, even unprecedented today, is that Catholic church leaders are speaking against U.S. Government policy. Rarely has this happened before.

Let me take just three issues which have received extensive media attention: The use of nuclear weapons, support for a specific human life amendment, and military spending in preference to social welfare programs. I would like to give a number of reasons for the apparently sudden change in the outspoken stands that bishops have taken:

1. Modern Popes have taken the lead. From Pope Leo XIII to the present charismatic leadership of Pope John Paul II popes have spoken clearly and forcefully on issues of social justice and peace. They have been outspoken in defense of the human person. This direction has been accepted and applied by bishops in their own countries.

2. The Second Vatican Council, for the first time in the history of the Church, gathered together bishops from the whole world including the developing nations. This gave them experience with dealing with issues beyond their individual national boundaries.

3. Since that Council, there has been a growing awareness that action for justice is a constitutive element of the preaching of the Gospel.

4. Many dioceses became personally involved in the Third World by accepting Pope John XXIII's call to send missionaries to Latin America. We came in touch with a source of accurate information about these countries. We also experienced poverty and injustice first hand.

5. Prior to the Second World War we had been a Church made up of immigrants. There was a deeply ingrained feeling among Catholics that we had to prove our loyalty to the government. We could be good Catholics and true Americans at the same time.

6. The civil rights struggles of the sixties began to involve many church leaders in demonstrating and speaking out against social sins. A social sin is a personal sin offensive to God that expresses itself in a structure or institution or in a way of thinking.

7. It was abortion that brought Catholic Church leaders in a direct confrontation with a national policy. We saw so clearly the need to change a way of thinking by applying our Christian teaching through education and action.

Jesus announced, "The reign of God is at hand. Reform your lives and believe in the gospel." (Mk 1,15) He wants to rule over our minds and hearts, over our families and communities and over every institution in our society. Jesus lives! He is risen! May he reign forever.

The Church In Brazil

Occasionally in our lifetimes we have experiences that change our lives. I had one of these when I was invited to make a trip to Brazil. I was on a study tour with a group of bishops, priests, sisters and representatives of labor unions. We went there to study the Church and the problems of the working people in Brazil, to give them support and encouragement, and to learn and apply the experiences of the trip to our own lives.

Brazil is a large country, bigger than the continental United States. We spent most of our time in and around the cities of Rio de Janeiro and Sao Paulo. Try to imagine the city of San Paulo with thirteen million inhabitants. It must be forty or fifty miles across.

Brazil is a country rich in natural resources and people, but poor in the distribution of its resources. Like so many other countries, it has huge gaps between the rich and the poor, a small percentage of the very rich owning the largest proportion of the productive wealth. The government, which is a military dictatorship, supports the rich and multi-national corporations in the exploitation of the poor.

Millions of farmers, mostly share-croppers and people with small holdings, have been forced off the land by large companies who then use the land for export crops such as lumber, sugar cane, bamboo and cattle. These vast numbers of people go to the cities looking to find work. If they can find work, they receive minimum salaries which are never enough for the basic necessities of life. Salaries are controlled by the government. With an inflation rate of 100%, even annual increases negotiated with the government do not keep up with the cost of living.

The labor unions are a vehicle of corporate government control. To organize and strike for higher wages is illegal and against national security. To stand with the poor is to be accused of communism and subversion.

Within all of this, the Church is one of the most alive churches in the world. Ever since the Latin American conferences at Medellin and Puebla, the Church has made an option for the poor. For hundreds of years church leadership in Brazil had been more allied with the privileged. Some of the bishops that we met told us of how they themselves went through a conversion, often after seeing the oppression of the poor and the use of torture against Christian leaders.

Cardinal Paulo Arns, Archbishop of Sao Paulo, declared that they were totally committed to non-violence. "Once violence begins," he said, "it will not end." To be committed to non-violence means that one has to do violence to oneself. There has to be a deep inner conviction that it is only through a change of heart and through the power of the Word of God that society can be changed.

Another bishop said: "The strength of the weak people lies not in the use of arms, but in unity." The Church is Brazil actively encourages the involvement of people in the life and ministry of the Church. Cardinal Arns said: "We must take seriously what God is doing through the Holy Spirit in his people." There is therefore, a great concentration on the development of what are called basic christian communities. These are small groups of perhaps ten to twenty families who meet every week to study the gospel, reflect on it, see its meaning in their lives, and work for the transformation of the world. Thousands of these small communities exist all over Brazil. I met with a number of them and with their leaders. They become a dynamic force in their neighborhoods, an element in building up God's reign in the world.

Every lent and advent, all throughout the Diocese of Sao Paulo, thousands and thousands of people meet in small groups with the guidance of materials prepared by the diocese after a great deal of consultation. Each week during these holy seasons, groups made up of couples, families, young people, elderly, meet to sing together, read from scriptures and share their faith and try to see how they can practically apply the Word of God to their daily lives. After doing this for a couple of seasons, many of the lenten groups want to continue to meet permanently, thus the basic christian communities are formed. They help to prepare their own children for the reception of the sacraments; they reach out to people in greater need than themselves; they work to get adequate sanitation facilities, water supplies, electricity in the slums in which they live; they meet to celebrate the Eucharist.

The whole Church in Brazil is committed to pastoral planning at every level, national, diocesan, regional and parish. With the involvement of a great number of people, the Diocese of Sao Paulo has identified six major goals: (1) visible unity, (2) evangelization, (3) catechesis, (4) the presence of the Church in the world, (5) liturgy, (6) ecumenism.

Every two years the pastoral plan is updated and specific objectives are developed for those two years, again with the participation of the people of the diocese.

There are so many other things that I could say about my trip. I was able to experience a dynamic church operating in the midst of almost insurmountable difficulties. Still they were optimistic since they truly believed that they were headed in the right direction and that they were led in this direction by the Holy Spirit.

As a church, we need to be more concerned about the transformation of the world, that is, we need to allow the Lord to rule over our lives and all aspects of our relationships with others. We too are living in a society with problems that seem to be so much bigger than we can deal with: the disregard for the lives of the unborn, widespread materialism and greed, unjust farm prices, the inability of young farmers to enter farming, the misuse of land, the growing concentration of wealth in the hands of a few, the arms race and the expenditure of vast sums for armaments.

It is only through a unified, faith-filled, committed people that we can begin to address these and many other questions of our society.

Greed

As a child, when I read the Bible story about the Israelites worshipping the golden calf, I wondered how it could be possible for people to do such a thing. Idol worship seemed so stupid. Anyone could see that the little statue was just a thing. It could not hear or speak, move or do anything, much less give life or happiness or forgiveness. How could anyone make it a god?

I knew from experience that I could turn against God in sin. I didn't see how I could possibly worship some thing made by human hands. Now I know differently. How easy it is to make idols out of things. We call it *greed*.

Greed is an immoderate love of possessing things and in particular, money. Jesus listed greed among those evils that "come from the deep recesses of the heart" along with acts of fornication, theft, murder, adulterous conduct, deceit, envy, blasphemy and arrogance. (Mk 7, 22-23)

Greedy or avaricious persons desire to possess things. They judge themselves in proportion to their wealth which they believe gives them value, prestige. Greedy people glory in their accumulations.

Actually, greed enslaves a person and makes him or her unhappy. St. John Chrysostom says, "Lust for money brings darkness on the soul when it puts out the light of charity by preferring the love of riches to the love of God." I suppose you are wondering what brought on all of this. Why is the Bishop suddenly so concerned about greed? I have been thinking about it for a long time. I am convinced that greed touches all of our lives.

Our society puts such a high value on possessing things. Now possessions as such are not evil. It is the "immoderate love" of them which is evil. They are gifts of God and we are stewards of them. We will have to give an account of how we use His gifts.

Remember that Jesus said, "Avoid greed in all its forms. A person may be wealthy, but his possessions do not guarantee him life" (Lk 12,15). Then Jesus went on to tell the story of the rich man who had a good harvest. He planned to build large grain bins and said to himself, "You have blessings in reserve for years to come. Relax! Eat heartily, drink well. Enjoy yourself."

Jesus concluded the story with these solemn words, "But God said to him, 'you fool! This very night your life shall be required of you. To whom will all this piled-up wealth of yours go?" (Lk 12, 20)

We all have to look at our own lives for evidence of greed. Do we have drawers and closets full of clothing we don't need? Do we buy gadgets and electrical appliances that we hardly ever use? Are we easily taken in by advertisements for the newest inventions that promise happiness, fulfillment, or beauty? What happened to last year's Christmas gifts that we gave to someone who "has everything?" When was the last time that we used the latest TV game that we thought we had to have? How much land do we really need? Is big really better? Do we need to expand? How much savings should we accumulate in order to provide for our old age? We are daily confronted with evidence of widespread poverty and injustice in the world. So much of it is a result of the greed of others. I know that I am affected by greed. I have to regularly ask myself how I use the good things that God has given me.

The opposite of greed is liberality, generosity. It is the good use of money or whatever has a monetary value. Liberality depends not on the amount given but on the heart of the giver. St. Thomas says that it tends to set in order one's own affection towards possessions and the use of money. He observes that the very act of liberally giving away one's possessions makes one happy.

Still, we all have to examine our motives. We give generously not because the parish or institution has a need. We give of our time, talent and treasures because we have a need to give. We have a need to be grateful to an all loving God who has given us life and an abundance of His blessings.

Conversion

I have discovered that the Lord does speak to me. What is more important, from my point of view, is that I hear him: during meditation, while reading the Scriptures, as I pray the liturgy of the hours, at Mass and at other times.

During meditation, I try to be very quiet, within and without. I breathe deeply and slowly. I put myself into the scene of a biblical story. I imagine I am there. I go beyond the scene. What do I see? What is he (or they) saying? What is he saying to me? What do I say or do? I jot down thoughts that come to me. I am convinced that this is a way that the Lord communicates to me in the depths of my being. It needs testing and discernment. That is why I submit it all openly to my spiritual director.

Faith, trust, amen, yes, repentance, reconciliation, conversion are all ways of saying the same thing: my response to God's call.

The root meaning of conversion is change of heart. If there is no response to God in my heart, in my whole being, I am not really a Christian.

I cannot be a Christian in mind only. Christianity is not just a doctrine or a system of beliefs. Christian life is Christ living in us and uniting each of us to the Father and to one another.

I cannot be a Christian in word only, for "what good is it to profess faith without practicing it?" (James 2,14). Christian life is the worship of God in Christ Jesus and the overflowing of that worship to love of my neighbor.

But I cannot be a Christian in action only either. Christianity is not just a set of duties and practices. Then I am just going through the motions.

The Lord calls us to a response of our total being. Faith leads to worship and worship leads to reaching out in loving concern to others and that in turn directs us back to God. It is an ever deepening spiral of love in response to a faithful, loving, merciful God.

Jesus began his public ministry with the words: "The reign of God is at hand! Reform your lives and believe in the good news!" (Mk 1, 14).

Conversion means turning around, "turning against" sin in our lives. How hard this is, especially when we do not even recognize our sin.

Conversion means change of heart, change from within.

Conversion means to "turn with," to turn with and walk with Jesus.

Conversion means to be reconciled, to be made one with God and each other. What a joy and privilege it is to receive the sacrament of reconciliation and hear the words "I absolve you from your sins" and to experience the pardon and peace of Jesus.

Conversion is not done once and for all. Conversion is for every day. It is saying "yes" to God daily. I must be converted over and over again.

Conversion is hearing God's call.

If Jesus is at the center of the Christian message, it is because he is the visible sign of the love and mercy of the Father calling us to conversion.

If evangelization is of the essence of the Church it is because evangelization is the process leading us to conversion.

If the Holy Eucharist is the source of the true Christian life it is because in the Body and Blood of Christ we are reconciled and made one with God and with each other.

Yes, conversion is at the center of the Christian life.

Civil Disobedience

I want to bring up an issue which is creating great interest today, namely, dissent from public policy and civil disobedience.

All of us know and accept the principle that any citizen in a democracy may disagree with an existing law and seek to have it changed. Our Christian sense may recognize that an existing policy is unfair or that it could be improved. It is our duty as citizens and as Christians to work for the passage of just laws.

So we are concerned about and work to change our laws affecting equitable taxation, human rights, abortion, land use, environmental pollution, prayer in the public schools, tax support for children attending parochial schools, and a host of other issues that touch our lives and beliefs.

We use peaceful and nonviolent means to get our ideas before the public and before our elected representatives. We write articles and letters, give speeches, participate in discussions, debates and conventions. We see that on most issues there can be legitimate differences of opinion. We work for consensus and compromise.

Now suppose a law or public policy is such that I cannot in conscience accept it. There are some issues on which, as a Catholic, as a follower of Jesus Christ, I cannot compromise. The policy of this country on abortion is wrong. We do not have to accept or participate in that policy.

There have been many instances in history where Catholics and other Christians disobeyed a law rather than violate their conscience. They used nonviolent means and were willing to pay the consequences. Frequently their witness was what got an unjust law or sinful public policy changed.

Early Christians were put to death rather than worship the Roman emperor as divine. They disobeyed civil law rather than their conscience.

When the empire disintegrated Christians were ready to bring a new life into Europe.

St. Thomas More, chancellor of England, would not support his king, Henry VIII when he declared himself head of the Church of England.

Many Polish people today engage in countless acts of nonviolent protest against a ruthless communist government. Dr. Martin Luther King and his followers disobeyed unjust laws, refusing to ride in the back of the bus, refusing to accept segregation in education, housing and public facilities. They went to jail. Some were beaten and killed. Through their nonviolent protest they brought about changes in a grave social evil.

Members of the Witnesses of Jehovah believe that saluting the flag is a violation of the First Commandment. They were beaten and jailed for refusing to obey a law requiring school children to salute the flag. Ultimately their position was upheld by the U.S. Supreme Court.

Hundreds of thousands of Americans are working to change the interpretation of the Constitution which allows abortions, taking life away from the unborn. We have a right to dissent. We must dissent. The issue is not going to go away.

Another issue which is not going to go away is the escalating arms race and the use of nuclear weapons in defense of our country.

The Church has consistently taught that acts of war deliberately directed against innocent noncombatants are gravely wrong. No one may participate in such an act. Thus a soldier would have to disobey orders if commanded to shoot civilians. No one could participate in obliteration bombing of cities. Here dissent would lead to disobedience, disobedience of human law in favor of obeying God's law. One can be a good Catholic and be a conscientious objector. That is, one has a right to object to all war and also the right to object to a particular war. This right is acknowledged by our government and protected by law, even though the government may demand some form of alternative community service.

There are some who refuse to pay their taxes on the grounds that their tax money is used for weapons and for war preparation. They are dissenting from a government policy. They are disobeying the law. They are ready to pay the consequences. I do not personally hold that position. But they do have the right to hold it. I thank them for their witness.

I believe that the arms race is evil and that among other things it is diverting valuable resources from the poor and from human services.

I believe that using nuclear weapons against civilian populations or threatening to so use them is evil. I believe that the very possession of nuclear weapons, as long as we are making no sustained commitment to achieve multilateral disarmament, is evil.

I do not want to contribute to this madness. What I do is take such a small salary that I no longer pay income tax. I make sure that my annual salary each year is no more than thirty-six hundred dollars. This is not a special hardship, my needs are few. I have no family to support. I am free to contribute to the poor.

Each of us in our own way must respond to the Lord's call. This is one way for me to do so.

Competition

We Americans are a competitive lot. Competition is in our bones. It is what keeps us moving. It is a style of life—part of the "American Way." We carved a nation out of diverse people and a wild untouched land.

I believe that competition is also killing us, destroying relationships, families and friends. It is part of our lives from little on. We are urged to compete. "Get ahead. Win. Be first. Get to the top."

There is an aspect of this that is good. I am not speaking against a little friendly competition in skill or ability or the challenge and fun of winning a game.

We should use the gifts that God has given us. That is the challenge from within us, to use our talents to the best of our ability to grow as well developed persons, to serve others and to worship God.

St. Paul uses the example of running a race: "I am racing to grasp the prize...My entire attention is on the finish line as I run toward the prize to which God calls me—life on high in Christ Jesus." (Phil. 3:12,14.) He speaks of fighting the good fight: "I have fought the good fight, I have finished the race, I have kept the faith. From now on a merited crown awaits me." (2 Tim. 4:7-8.)

I am against the kind of competition that is an all consuming goal, that means getting ahead no matter what it does to anyone else. It is sometimes even competition to the death. It is an unhealthy rivalry.

One of the bishops from the Minnesota iron range said that the head of one of the steel companies told him, "Can't you do something to help the people in this community understand that it is all over. We cannot open the mine again. Competition has killed us." One company "won" over another. It became first. What about all those people now out of work? What effects

87

does it have on families? On a community? We have come to accept the answer, "business is business."

A few short years ago, a multinational company bought out Green Giant Company in Le Sueur. A short time later it pulled out of its executive, administrative and research departments, leaving behind only a canning operation in the community. Profitability, competition became the overriding factors in the decision to move. What about people? What about the contribution of a community over a period of many years? Examples could be multiplied in town after town in all parts of the country.

Competition drives us to keep up with the neighbors. It is often tinged with envy, avarice and greed. Competition often enters into our decision to buy new cars or increased acreage, not to speak of recreational equipment, clothing, records, books, even cosmetics.

Look at how competition has entered into school sports. Again, I am not speaking against a little healthy competition or developing a strong and supple body. I support a well-rounded physical education program where all children and youth can participate to the extent of their ability and where there is a balance of mental, physical, emotional and spiritual development in a school.

The all-consuming competition of professional sports has worked its way down through college sports, to high school and grade school and even to the pee-wees.

There is something wrong, I think, when a town is identified only by its high school team. There is something wrong when a college football coach is paid many times more than an excellent professor of English or history or philosophy. We are mixing up our values when only a few can participate and when winning is the all-important value. There is something wrong when little kids are roused from bed before sunrise in order to get ice time for hockey practice.

Competition continues in our national policies. We are number one. We dominate in economic and military might. We want everyone to be like us, to accept our way. How many times have we sent troops to protect our interests in Central America and elsewhere during the last twenty-five years? I can't even count them.

A striving for power can affect us in the Church also. Yet, Jesus teaches us to serve, to love one another, to give, to be last, to become as little children, to turn the other cheek, to forgive. That is the message, the unpopular message, that we proclaim.

Sexual Responsibility

I write this especially for young people. Parents and teachers, if the young people in your life are not likely to read this, I ask you to read it to them and discuss it at the supper table, in the classroom or in the parish youth group.

My topic is pre-marital sexual intercourse or sexual relations between a man and a woman, neither of whom is married. It is technically called fornication.

A prevailing attitude in our society is that such activity is all right. It is even considered good as long as the two people care for each other and do it freely. "Make your own decision," they are told.

Teenagers are told that sexual intercourse is okay for them if they really like one another, if no one gets hurt and if means are taken not to become pregnant. This is a message they hear from the entertainment industry, from their friends, even in their health or physical education classes.

Planned Parenthood Association spends millions of dollars every year teaching young people all about birth control on the assumption that sexual activity is going to take place among unmarried young people and that it is perfectly all right to do so. If birth control fails, abortion clinics are readily available to destroy the unborn babies.

Lord God, what have we come to! You have shown us the way to life and happiness and we have chosen selfishness and death.

Jesus said, "Wicked designs come from the deep recesses of the heart; acts of fornication, theft, murder, adulterous conduct, greed, maliciousness, deceit,...All these evils come from within and render a man or woman impure." (Mk 7:21- 22)

And St. Paul forcefully writes, "Make no mistake about this: no fornicator, no unclean or lustful person—in effect an idolator—has any inheritance in the kingdom of Christ or of God. Let no one deceive you with worthless arguments. These are sins that bring God's wrath down on the disobedient; therefore, have nothing to do with them." (Eph 5:5-6)

The above are but two of the dozen or more passages from the Bible that clearly speak on this subject. The Christian message about sex and sexuality is a positive, beautiful one.

Fornication is evil, sinful because it makes a mockery out of sex which is a God-given power of transmitting life.

Sex, our human sexuality, is holy. It makes us God-like. The Bible describes it in this way: "Then God said: 'Let us make man in our image, after our likeness'...God created man in his image; in the divine image he created him; male and female he created them." (Gen 1:26-27) We are like God not only in that we can think and choose—that is, in our spirit. We are also like God in our bodies, in our sexuality. We share with God himself the power to create, to give life. Men and women are given the awesome gift of bringing into the world other human beings who are also called to eternal life.

Sexual union is holy, beautiful, life-giving and joyful in marriage where two people have freely committed themselves to one another for life. Intercourse is a sign of total human giving. Sexual union outside a permanent total commitment is not responsible. It becomes recreational sex, selfish sex, sex for fun and without responsibility.

I know how hard it is for young people to be different from their friends. The pressures are enormous to act like everyone else. "Everyone is doing it," they say. That is simply not true. Still it is hard to stand up for what one knows is right.

Chastity in our society is laughed at. Fidelity in marriage is ridiculed. "Living together" before marriage has become common.

In order to be chaste, it is not only necessary to say "no" to sexual relations outside of marriage, it is also necessary to say "no" to those thoughts, words and activities that lead to it: our manner of dress, going steady when we are not ready for marriage, spending long periods of time together exclusively and alone.

The words of St. Paul summarize the stand of the Christian, the follower of Christ: "Do you not see that our bodies are members of Christ?...The fornicator sins against his own body. You must know that your body is a temple of the Holy Spirit, who is within—the Spirit you have received from God. You are not your own. You have been purchased, and at a price! So glorify God in your body." (1Cor 6:15-20).

Evangelization

I sit at my desk reflecting on a trip I made to our diocesan mission in San Lucas Toliman, Guatemala. I was accompanied by two of my nieces, one a senior in High School, the other a sophomore in College. Both of them speak Spanish and went to learn about and experience poverty and development in the third world.

I found the situation in Guatemala much more calm than it has been in previous years. Although we heard reports of clashes with guerillas in the north and west, we saw almost no government soldiers during our week-long stay.

I always come back from the mission with a deep sense of pride for the work that is being done there. With great dedication, our priests, sisters and lay volunteers continue to give of themselves totally and without remuneration. They could not do their work without the support and prayers of the people of the Diocese of New Ulm.

I visited the Catholic grade school in San Lucas—overcrowded, bulging at the seams with over six hundred pupils. I celebrated Mass with them and shared their faith, their joy and their enthusiasm. Our presence in San Lucas has helped to reduce the illiteracy rate there from over ninety-five percent twenty years ago to fifteen percent today.

The orphanage houses and lovingly cares for over one hundred children, many of them victims of violence. It is called Casa Feliz (Happy House), and that is what it is in spite of the pain and sorrow that so many of them have experienced.

A highlight of the week was a trip to the neighboring town of Santiago Atitlan where Father Stan Rother was murdered. We went there at the invitation of the people of Santiago and their new pastor to thank Father Greg Schaffer and John Goggin for their devoted service to that com-

93

munity for the last three years. In addition to their already heavy load at San Lucas, two or three times a week they made the back- wrenching, bone-crunching and often dangerous trips by four- wheel drive vehicle to Santiago to celebrate Mass and administer the sacraments.

It was a glorious celebration with two or three thousand Indian people jamming the church, all in traditional dress. Men with purple and white stripped short pants with colorful woven sashes. Women in beautiful, colorful handwoven skirts and blouses with a unique crown on their heads made of long bands of bright red ribbon.

The people of Santiago presented me with a handwoven stole specifically precious to them because it was in Father Stan's possession when he was killed. It was given as a sign of appreciation for our priests. I was deeply moved.

Another highlight of the trip was a visit to a newly acquired two hundred acre piece of land which is to be divided into two or three acre plots and made available to poor landless people. This land has been made available by a Presbyterian Church group in Indianapolis plus a bequest from a person in the Diocese of New Ulm. To see the joy and the hope on the faces of people who were looking forward to a little place of their own brought tears to my eyes. They join the thirteen hundred other families from the area who have been able to purchase their own land with the help of friends of San Lucas. It is one of the reasons why San Lucas Toliman remains an "island of peace" in a violence-torn country.

During my trip I spent several hours reading a beautiful book on spirituality by Gustavo Gutierrez, *We Drink From Our Own Wells.* "A Christian," he says, "is defined as a follower of Jesus." A follower of Jesus is a disciple. A disciple is invited to share in the life, death and resurrection of Jesus. Spirituality has to do with living the life of God and growing in a relationship with him. As a son or daughter of God, each person has an inalienable human dignity. Thus discipleship, following Jesus, spirituality, living according to the Spirit of life and love and walking in freedom are all related.

One comes to be a disciple of Jesus by the grace of God and the witness of another believer or community of believers. And one cannot be a true believer unless his or her faith leads to good works. As Gutierrez puts it— "There is no authentic envangelization that is not accompanied by action on behalf of the poor."

Evangelization has two aspects: handing on the faith on the part of the witness and coming to faith on the part of the one who is converted. Both are moved by the grace of God. And both must express their faith by living it out in action on behalf of the poor, the powerless, the sick, the lonely.

It is of the very essence of the Church that each of us seeks to bring the Good News of Salvation to all people everywhere. Pope Paul VI wrote, "Evangelization is in fact the grace and vocation proper to the Church, her deepest identity. She exists in order to evangelize."

We are in Guatemala to evangelize. The first task of every parish is to evangelize. The primary responsibility of parents is to evangelize. In each case we are witnesses, we are instruments through which people, moved by the grace of God, say "yes" to God and to all that he has revealed.

Again quoting Pope Paul VI, "Evangelization means bringing the Good News into all the strata of humanity, and through its influence transforming humanity from within and making it new."

Essential to evangelization is interior change on the part of the witness and on the part of the recipient.

A Hoe and a Hammer

While I was in San Lucas Toliman, Guatemala, in 1984 something happened to me which touched me deeply. It was about a hoe.

A Guatemalan farmer has two basic tools—a hoe and a machete. He uses the hoe to plow, to cultivate, to hill beans and corn, dig, mix cement, load a wheelbarrow. It is a versatile implement. So is the machete, which is a large, heavy knife with a broad blade used for trimming trees, cutting vegetation, harvesting sugar cane or corn and similar uses.

The hoe is unlike our own. The blade is heavy, made of cast steel about eleven inches wide and eight inches high. It has a circle of steel on the upper edge through which a handle, a branch of a coffee tree, is inserted, more like a pick or a mattock. Heavy, and worked with a steady rhythm, it is an efficient tool.

For a Guatemalan a hoe is a substantial investment. One costs around fifteen dollars. Saving up for one a nickel or a dime at a time may take several years. It is not unlike a farmer in this country purchasing his first tractor.

I thought I would like to buy one of these fine tools for myself. I could use it in the garden. Only I didn't want to buy a new one. After they are used for several years they wear down to almost half their original size. I figured that it wouldn't be quite so heavy for me to use.

I asked Fr. Greg, one of the missionaries from our diocese, "Do you suppose that you could find someone who would be willing to give me his old worn hoe, if I bought him a new one?" A couple of days later he said, "I think I made you a deal. Aquilino Yoxon, with some reluctance, is willing to trade." His reluctance, it turned out, was based on the idea that he believed that it was unjust to me. I was getting his old worn hoe and he was getting a new one. Fr. Greg said, "But the Bishop insists that he buy you a new one. After all, he really wants a worn one." He finally agreed when he came up with the idea that he would make me a new handle. Then both of us had something new.

But the story doesn't stop there. Whenever we go to Guatemala we try to bring along some extra boxes filled with blankets, children's clothing, medicine and other things that are so desperately needed by the mission. These are things that cannot be shipped or mailed in since the import tax is so high. We carry them in as part of our luggage.

In one of the boxes I placed four new steel shanked hammers. Someone had brought them in some time ago hoping that they could be used by someone in Guatemala.

After the deal was made with Aquilino, Fr. Greg gave him one of the hammers. He took it in his work-toughened hands, looked at Father and said gratefully, "I have been saving up to buy a hammer since 1976."

Imagine. Eight years! Ever since the earthquake when so much rebuilding had to be done in the area, he tried to buy a simple tool. We cannot even imagine it. We have extra hammers (along with wrenches, screwdrivers and pliers) in the kitchen drawer, in the car and several in the shop and other locations around the place.

Aquilino Yoxon, a poor landless Indian farmer, teaches me so much about poverty and injustice, dignity and honor, and the value of simple things that we so take for granted.

Equal Rights
Amendment

The Equal Rights Amendment to the United States Constitution was passed by Congress in 1972 and sent on to the states for ratification. It needs to be ratified by three more states before the deadline of June 30, 1982.

The amendment declares that "equality of rights under the law shall not be denied or abridged by the United States or by any state on account of sex" and that "the Congress shall have the power to enforce, by appropriate legislation, the provisions of this article."

The debate and controversy over the adoption of the Equal Rights Amendment have been long and intense. Many people have asked me to take a position on it.

Last fall I joined with Bishop Balke in publishing a pastoral letter on Christian feminism. We described Christian feminism as an attitude of mind and heart that recognizes in the light of the Gospel that women are equal because they share the same humanity, are created in the divine image by God, are redeemed by Jesus Christ, are called to the same holiness and through the gifts of the Spirit have a rightful place in the life and mission of the Church.

We described sexism as the erroneous belief that one sex, female or male, is superior to the other in the very order of creation. We declared that when anyone believes that men are inherently superior to women or that women are inherently superior to men, then he or she is guilty of sexism, a moral and social evil.

I have a thick file of letters in response to our pastoral letter. All but two or three were in support of our position. Some asked me, "Now, what is your position on the proposed Equal Rights Amendment?"

I want to state again that equal rights for women is part of the Christian message.

God created men and women in his own image. He gave them dominion over all creatures.

Jesus in a radical departure from the accepted practices of his day associated with women, taught them, healed them, counted them among his followers and supporters. The faithful women were present at the cross and were the first witnesses to the Resurrection.

Make no mistake about it: equal rights for all flows from the very message of Jesus. St. Paul writes, "There does not exist among you Jew or Greek, slave or freeman, make or female. All are one in Christ Jesus." (Gal. 3:28)

Pope Paul VI specifically supported "winning equal rights for women" as one of the aims of the International Women's Year in 1975. The task, he emphasized is "to endeavor everywhere to bring about the discovery of, respect for, and protection of the rights and prerogatives of every women, single or married, in education, in the professions, and in civil, social and religious life." (Address to the Committee for the International Women's Year, April 18, 1975)

The proposed Equal Rights Amendment to the Constitution is seen by its supporters as a way to bring about equal rights and protection to women in the United States. Any change in the Constitution is accompanied by risks, even dangers. One cannot know in advance how it will be interpreted by the courts. Considering the advantages and the dangers, one makes a political decision on the light of the text of the amendment itself, its legislative history, the opinions of constitutional scholars and others who have studied the issue in the light of the Gospel.

One can be a good Catholic and be either for or against the Equal Rights Amendment. One cannot be a good Catholic and be against equal rights for women.

Many Catholic organizations and individuals have taken public positions against the Equal Rights Amendment, among them the National Council of Catholic Women, the Knights of Columbus and the Daughters of Isabella. They believe that the ERA could lead to all sorts of evils and in particular that it could give constitutional support for abortion.

In being against the ERA they are accused by some as being opposed to equal rights for women. That is unfair. The Council of Catholic Women, for example, has a record of working for the advancement of women's rights especially through legislation.

Other Catholic groups are working for the adoption of the Equal Rights Amendment, including the National Conference of Catholic Charities, the Leadership Conference of Women Religious, the Conference of Major Superiors of Men, and the National Federation of Priests' Councils. They believe that it will advance equal rights for women. They are accused of being in favor of abortion. This is unfair. Catholics in favor of ERA see no connection between the amendment and abortion.

Most bishops have made no public statement either for or against the Equal Rights Amendment. They correctly see it as an issue on which each person has to weigh the evidence and make a decision in the light of his or her own conscience.

I believe strongly in equal rights for women. I am for Christian feminism. That flows from my faith in Jesus and on his life and teaching.

After studying the issue, after much reflection and discussion, I am personally in favor of the Equal Rights Amendment. I am convinced that it would promote equal dignity and justice for women in our society. I am not persuaded that it would allow or promote abortion. If I thought that I would be opposed to the amendment.

I do not claim this as official Catholic teaching. Nor do I wish to impose it on others. I am speaking from my own heart.

Gardening—A Meditation

I have been gardening almost as long as I can remember. I watched and later helped my father as he pursued his annual task. He sowed seeds in homemade flats. As the seedlings emerged he put them on windowsills to catch the sun, watered them using a tin can punctured in the bottom with small nail holes, transplanted them into a cold frame and finally set them in the garden.

I remember tomatos and petunias, salvias and snapdragons transplanted this way from bedding plants. Other seeds were planted directly into the garden—lettuce, radishes, onions, beets, carrots, zinnias, marigolds and finally dahlias. My, what dahlias. They were huge and they were beautiful.

He tried to stretch a meager depression salary with fresh vegetables. He swept manure by the sackful from railroad stock cars and saved his own seed from the best specimens year to year. His garden was the prettiest and most productive in the neighborhood. Bouquets of fresh cut flowers regularly graced our table.

I was only thirteen when he died. Somehow I felt it was my responsibility to keep the garden going. I did for a few years. By then I was in the Seminary and we had to stay in school all summer during the World War II years.

For the last fifteen years or so I have had a big garden every year. Eight of us live in the community at the Pastoral Center. With canning, freezing and storing, the garden supplies almost all of our vegetables for the year. It is the middle of April and we still have potatoes and squash in the garage and bags of carrots in the refrigerator from last year. The onions and rhubarb are finished. Many packages of peas, beans, corn, asparagus, peppers, applesauce and strawberries will hold us until the next crop comes in.

Gardening is a meditation.

It teaches me how precious life is. The soil is a living thing that needs to be nourished, enriched with organic matter, handed on in as good or better condition than when we received it. The soil of our nation is best cared for through widespread distribution of land in a family farm system.

I am reminded of the good soil that Jesus talked about—the receptive and sincere person who receives the word of God. The word finds a fertile place to grow and the family, the community and the world are blessed.

I learn something of God's love for me as I gather the abundant harvest. I learn that the soil and the food that comes from it is a gift, that everyone has a right to food, that food must never be used as a political weapon.

I think about our forebears who homesteaded the rich prairie soil, established towns and parish communities. All this is threatened by the rural crisis and the growing tendency in our country to concentrate land in the hands of a few.

I reflect on how everything about food, its production, storage, preparation and eating, is meant to be a community thing. As soon as any aspect of it becomes turned in on itself, selfish or individualistic, it becomes less human and more dominated by seekers of power.

The very process of growth is for me a deep meditation about the meaning of life and death. "Unless the grain of wheat falls to the earth and dies," Jesus said, "it remains just a grain of wheat. But if it dies, it produces much fruit." (Jn 12, 24). The very center of our faith is that Jesus died and rose again so that we also may live forever.

Wisdom And Courage

One of the best things I do all year is conduct official visitations of our parishes. It takes a whole weekend. I visit the Catholic school, if there is one; I meet with teachers and catechists. I spend time listening to and supporting the parish staff; I speak with the parish council, committees, boards and organizations; I visit the shut-ins and anoint the sick; I participate in and speak at the parish liturgies; and I administer the sacrament of Confirmation.

A heavy weekend, it usually leaves me exhausted. It also gives me a lift as I see and experience the wonderful things that God is doing among His people and the various ways that they are responding to His gifts.

One weekend in 1985 as I was about to celebrate Mass with the children, one of the servers, a well-trained sixth grader, asked me, "Is there anything that you want us to do?" I replied, "No, but since this is a special school Mass, I may need your help to tell me what I need to do."

A little third grader stood on a stool to reach the microphone and beautifully read the first reading. As she was heading back to her place, the server tugged on my sleeve and whispered, "You're supposed to say, 'This is the word of the Lord.'"

The most moving experience for me that weekend was the Confirmation of Megan McGraw. At the time, Megan was a remarkable ninth grader. The previous February she had broken her back while sliding on a hill and was now paralyzed from the waist down. She wanted to be confirmed with her class. After the accident, and months of pain, frustration, surgery and rehabilitation, and just one day out of the hospital she joined the procession into the church in her wheelchair.

Each of the Confirmation candidates made an individually composed profession of faith as he or she was presented for the sacrament. They spoke from their hearts. When Megan's turn came she spoke clearly into the microphone, "I believe in God because He has made Himself specially evident in these past months. I have always believed in God because my parents taught me, but now through personal experience I feel I know God and how wonderfully caring He is. I know He will help me make my life important." The church was hushed.

When she came up to be anointed with Holy Chrism and "sealed with the gift of the Holy Spirit," I was suddenly moved to step close to her and say, "I am going to pray especially that you receive the gifts of wisdom and courage. I believe that the Lord has a special task for you to do."

I don't know why I was moved to say that. It had never happened before. Tears came to my eyes and I had a hard time to go on. The gift of wisdom enables one to see things as God sees them. The gift of courage gives one the ability to do what should be done.

Some Things I Can't Fix

I grew up in a family of fixers.

My father could fix or make anything. He had a rack of tools, kept sharp and in order. He repaired the plumbing and electrical fixtures and painted the house. He had a large garden, saving seeds and bulbs from year to year and growing his own bedding plants.

He built child-sized kitchen tables and chairs and make-believe appliances for my sisters. He even serviced and repaired his own cars—Model A Fords at first and then his pride and joy, a new 1936 Chevrolet.

I remember that Chevrolet had three models that year: standard, master and master deluxe. We got a master. Not the cheapest. Not the best either. It was a black, four-door sedan. We were proud of it. With a little squeezing all eight of us could go in it for our regular Sunday visits to relatives. It also is the basis for my life-long belief that Chevies must be better than Fords.

Anyway, my father was great fixer. My mother was too. She baked bread and marvelous coffee cakes. She canned, made jellies, jams and pickles. There was nothing like her cooking: cakes from scratch, soups, dumplings.

She made her own dresses and clothes for my sisters. She sewed drapes and upholstered furniture.

My aunts and uncles were the same way. I used to work at my uncle's farm during the summer time. There wasn't anything that he couldn't make or repair with a few boards or pieces of iron and with the aid of some baling wire, nails and bolts.

So you see I come into fixing honestly. I am from a family of fixers.

As I grew up, however, I found that there were some things that they could not fix. Like the depression. My parents couldn't fix that. But they taught us how to live with it and to help others who were worse off than we were. My father joined Father Coughlin's crusade and delivered his tabloid newspaper "The Social Justice Review."

They couldn't change the impending war, World War II.

My mother couldn't change my father's death. I was always angry with him because he died so young. He was only forty-two and I was just entering the eighth grade. My mother helped us cope with that grief, giving us strength and hope.

I have learned also that there are some things that I can't fix. Those of us in caring professions are constantly trying to help people in times of crisis. People come to us for counseling, for help in resolving family conflicts, for advice.

We can help. With the grace of God and with the gifts that we are given, the Lord touches people. They feel better. Their problems are resolved. They are reconciled, healed, forgiven.

But there are so many things that I can't fix. Sometimes people have such unrealistic expectations. They think that if I just write a letter to all of the pastors, if I just tell people what to do, if I just make this visit, write a letter, talk to a certain person their concern will be taken care of, their problem solved.

People sometimes expect me to solve a conflict between a pastor and certain parishioners, between a board of education and a parish council, between a principal and a teacher. I or my staff may be able to help. But basically the parties must deal with the issue together, perhaps with a facilitator or a judge.

When an issue is more complex and involves many factors, it is all the more difficult to work out a solution unless many people work together with a determined effort.

Here are some problems which some people expect me to do something about: a parish suffering a crushing debt, a school facing a threat of closing, farm families about to lose their farm, a community struggling with survival, a nation collapsing from within, due to abortion, failing family life, so much violence and an arms race out of control.

These are issues which I cannot fix. None of them can be dealt with by anyone alone. They call for community action, working and praying together.

Society, yes the whole world can be changed. But only as each one of us changes in his or her own heart and as we join together.

Above all we need to rely on the grace and power of God.

Going Back To Our Roots

In the summer of 1985 I went back to my roots. I traveled Germany and Luxembourg with my sister to visit the towns where my grandparents came from.

We had the special joy of staying with a second cousin and his wife, Maximilian and Gisela Lucker (spelled Luecker in Germany). Their home is in Bruehl, a suburb of Cologne. Max's grandfather and my grandfather were brothers. They welcomed us, fed us and cared for us, drove us around, saw to our every need. They were so kind and loving it was almost overwhelming.

We visited the beautiful Eifel mountain region of Germany, near the Luxembourg and Belgium borders. There we went to the town of Dahnen where my grandfather was born and the nearby town of Daleiden where he retired before he died. We visited some other cousins in Daleiden, ate some of their home-smoked ham and talked about our mutual backgrounds.

We drove to the village of Gilsdorf in Luxembourg where my mother's family came from. There we were warmly received and had a wonderful meal at the home of relatives.

I write about this because I believe that it is so important to keep in touch with our roots, to remember and to see the hand of God in our history.

Our memories tend to go back no more than two or three generations. We remember our grandparents and have only vague and dim snippets of information about our great-grandparents. We usually cannot go beyond that. If there are any old pictures around, they are unmarked and no one can identify the people anymore. What a pity! Isn't it a shame that we forget where we come from? We forget the joys and sorrows, the success and failures of those very people who have been such a part of our lives.

One of the most valued treasures in our family is a picture taken at my Aunt Mamie's wedding in 1903. There in front of the old homestead are some eighty-five relatives: parents, grandparents, brothers and sisters, uncles and aunts and cousins of the bride and groom. My mother, now eighty-six, is one of the few people still alive who was present on that happy day.

There is a woman in the picture proudly holding a wedding cake. "Oh, that's Aunt Katie Rettner. She always baked the cakes," my mother informs me. "Who is this little girl?" I ask. "She was another Katie. Katie Pabst. She died as a young girl. I remember going to her funeral." Who was that? "He was the school teacher."

It is good to hear these stories and to recall God's presence in all of them.

As I read the Bible I recall that it is the story of God's love and how He revealed Himself to a people. He guided them, rescued them from slavery, fed them, gave them a land, taught them and chastised them. Above all He sent His Son who lived among them and us to teach us, unite us with his grace, heal us and redeem us.

The stories of the Old Testament were handed down for hundreds of years before their final collection and editing. In all of it the prophets and writers saw the hand of God.

We need to do the same thing. We need to recall the past, and with the eyes of faith see God's loving presence in our family history.

With a little reflection we can write the story of our lives as a story of God's presence in our lives and of our response to that presence. We can say, "this is how I met my husband or wife. God was present in our marriage and at the birth of our children. He has been present at every step of the way."

Many of us can see the hand of God even in a tragedy, sickness and death. We go beyond the story and say, "That was when I really felt God's love in so many helpful people. That was when I came to know the Lord."

We need to look back and see the action of God in our families when they chose to immigrate and settle in this land. We recognize God's love as they struggled to homestead unbroken land or practice a trade, as their children and their children's children were born, sought an education, went to war and became leaders in our communities. God was with them.

I live in a community of priests and sisters where every year we tell each other the story of our faith. We share our lives, our struggles and our gifts and how God uses us in our weakness and sinfulness to touch the lives of others.

As we share our stories and tell of God's presence in them, we become witnesses and instruments through which God touches the hearts of other people to respond in faith and love in their own lives.

Tell your story. Recall your family history. Remember your roots and praise God.

Thoughts About Death

Some of the most intensely moving religious experiences come to us in times of pain, suffering and grief. In loneliness too; yes, and even in guilt. God can be present also in moments of great joy: at weddings, at the birth of a baby, at meals, at the gathering of friends, in intimate expressions of friendship and love.

Death especially brings us in touch with the divine.

My first experience of death was when I couldn't have been much older than seven. A little girl up the street died suddenly of pneumonia. I remember how all of us children on the block, maybe twenty or so at the time, walked two by two to the wake at her house where we prayed the rosary.

A couple of years later my grandfather died. He had come over from Luxembourg as a child with his family. He was kind, loved children and in his old age did a few chores around my uncle's farm. I was not quite ten and was learning the Latin prayers in preparation for being a server. At my grandfather's funeral I served for the first time.

One of the most traumatic and influential experiences of my life was the death of my father. He died quickly and without warning in the middle of the night, at the age of forty-two, the day before I began the eighth grade.

I remember every moment: being awakened by my worried and grief-stricken mother, being sent with my sister to bring my Uncle Pete who lived a couple of blocks away. He would know what to do. My older brother was sent over to the Smiths, neighbors across the street, to use the phone to call the priest. It was the depression and we could not afford a telephone.

These early experiences of death were times of grace as well as wonder and pain. I learned about the reality of death and through a faith-filled family, relatives, neighbors and friends I experienced the goodness and love of God. I came to know something about the finality of death. But even more, I was given the grace to believe that death was not the end, that "life is not ended but changed" to something more glorious.

Gradually my faith told me that God is not a God of death but of life. God does not want death but life. In the Risen Lord Jesus we are all one in faith, in hope and in the call to everlasting glory.

As Catholics we believe in the judgment of God; we believe that we will have to give an account of our lives as Jesus so graphically reminded in his teaching about the sheep and the goats. We believe also in purgatory, a place of temporary separation from God for those who are not quite ready for heaven and not deserving of hell. Catholic theology speaks of temporal punishment due for sin.

So we pray for the dead, especially during November, the month of the Holy Souls. We are all members of the Communion of Saints.

Everytime I offer Mass I remember my father, my grandparents, my uncles and aunts, my relatives and friends who have died. I pray for my priest classmates, the priests, religious and people who have gone before us marked with the sign of faith.

Conscientious Objection

I support the right of a young man (the law only affects men at this time) to be a conscientious objector. Conscientious objection means that someone is sincerely opposed to participation in any war because of religious, moral or ethical belief. This right of conscientious objection is a valid moral position for a Catholic. It is derived from the Gospel and Catholic teaching. Moreover, it is recognized in United States law.

Some have accused me of not being patriotic because I want to help young people know their legal rights regarding to draft registration and conscientious objection. I am a patriotic American. I am proud of my country. I love my country. I want our country to be strong and free. I believe that strength has to come from within, from a people who are generous and caring, just and forgiving, honest and truthful, faithful and kind.

A nation is judged on how it cares for its weakest citizens: the poor and the homeless, the handicapped and the exploited, the unborn and the elderly, the young and the uneducated.

One who is patriotic has the right and indeed the duty of try to strengthen our country. Not everything that we do as a people is right. Consider abortion. I must criticize and work to change that terrible public policy.

Consider the farm crisis. I must work to change present government policies which are unjust to family farmers.

Consider pornography and a wide range of other moral issues which cry out for public policies which will make our country stronger.

I do not consider opposition to present government positions as un-patriotic.

Let me make my position clear. In the case of conscientious objection I ask our schools, religious education teachers, pastors, counselors, parish workers and parents to instruct young men who must register for the draft about their options.

When a young man reaches his eighteenth birthday, he must register. Some have said that I advise young people not to register. I do not advise or support that way of acting. Moreover, a heavy fine and jail sentence can be imposed for not registering.

We are told by military planners themselves that in a few years volunteers will not be sufficient to meet the manpower needs of the military services. At that time the draft will be put into effect and young men will be called by their draft boards to report for physical exams and induction into the military. A person has only ten days to make his claim of conscientious objection, if that is his position, known to the government.

What advice do I give you if you object sincerely and religiously to war? I would tell you that you have a legal right to be a conscientious objector. But you have to document your case. And you should begin early to gather evidence of your sincerity and your religious and moral convictions.

You could, for example, write somewhere on your registration form that you are a conscientious objector, even though there is no space for it.

You could register with a national group like the Pax Christi Center on Conscience and War (Box 726, Cambridge, MA 02139). This is not only objective evidence of your sincerity, you will find there a valuable resource for information on the subject.

You should keep a record of meetings and seminars attended, discussions, television shows, books and other things that have influenced your decision to morally oppose war. You should note any peace activities, other humanitarian or volunteer work you have done.

It is important to be able to show how the Church and its teaching has influenced you. You will need letters of support from teachers, clergy, counselors and parents. Special attention may be given to persons who disagree with your position but who know you to be sincere.

Above all, it is important to talk to a counselor, one whom you know and trust and who is knowledgeable about draft counseling.

You should also know that if you are granted conscientious objector status you will be required to give some alternate service for the same number of years that you would have been required to serve in the military.

I also support those who serve their country in military service. We need to give them support and love and moral guidance according to the Bishops' Pastoral Letter on War and Peace. We also have to help them make difficult decisions before they go into military service.

Work And The Family

In March, 1986, I participated in a three-day theological symposium on Christian marriage at the University of Dayton in Ohio. There were eight of us on the panel of speakers: theologians, a scripture scholar, a psychiatrist and a canon lawyer. Five of the speakers were married people, three of them women. The other three were priests.

We dealt with difficult issues. My role was to reaffirm the official teachings of the Church on matters such as contraception, pre-marital and extra-marital sexual relations, and the indissolubility of sacramental and consummated marriage.

I was also there to listen to what theologians, counselors and married people are saying, and to translate these teachings into the world of today and the twenty-first century.

We believe that with the help of the Holy Spirit there is a continual development of doctrine in the Church. That is, there is a growth in the understanding of the tradition that comes from the apostles. "This happens," the Second Vatican Council taught, "through the contemplation and study made by believers who treasure these things in their hearts. The Church constantly moves forward toward the fullness of divine truth until the words of God reach their fulfillment in her." (Revelation, 8)

While truths of faith never change, our theological understanding of them does. And sometimes we find that what we thought was of faith, was in fact not. All theological formulations are bound up in expressions that are conditioned by culture and time.

For a long time, for example, theologians in the church taught that sexual relations in marriage were at least venially sinful. The Vatican Council made a major leap forward in clearly teaching that sexual expression in marriage is good. Indeed, the sacrament of marriage is lived most fully in sexual lovemaking. For in our human sexuality we are created in God's image. And in its chaste use God is praised and worshipped.

One of the most significant areas of agreement during the symposium by almost all of the speakers was that we (the Church) need to call on, listen to, and invite reflection on the experience of married persons.

There has been a veritable explosion of people accepting the call and the challenge to exercise ministries of all kinds within the Church.

Where we have not done so well is in recognizing, affirming, and supporting people in the transformation of the world, which is essentially the ministry of the laity.

By "we" I speak of bishops and church leaders. We have encouraged people in teaching ministries, youth work, pastoral care, liturgical ministries, spiritual direction, ministries of concern for the poor, the widow, peace and justice; but all of this within the Church and under Church leadership and control.

Yet the Second Vatican Council said, "The laity, by their vocation, seek the kingdom of God by engaging in temporal affairs, and by ordering them according to the plan of God."

It is especially in the family and in society, in sexuality and marriage, in economics and in work that the transformation of the world must take place.

The symposium helped me to clarify my thoughts on this.

There is a parallel in history between the way we (white males, especially) treat the land (and sea and sky) and the way we treat women. I use land to include the whole field of economics, the world. And I use the word "woman" here to include sexuality, fertility, sexual relationship.

Land is looked upon as a commodity to be used, owned, exploited, dominated. Women are similarly considered.

Land could be bought, sold, discarded. Land is an object of our greed, our covetousness. Women are also.

When women are degraded or exploited, sexuality is rejected as sacred, good, beautiful, powerful, to be treated with respect and responsibility.

Our land, our water, our air are being contaminated, used up, polluted through greed and exploitation and contaminated by chemicals and nuclear fallout. Economic injustice results when a few can lay claim to absolute ownership and exploitation of the goods of the earth.

Human sexuality is degraded when it is trivialized, when people treat one another as sex objects, when there is little commitment.

I see so many connections between pollution of soil, water and land, and sexual exploitation; between economic repression and preparations for war; between the rejection of God in the world of work and the rejection of God in human sexuality.

Yes, every member is called to transform the world. And that is particularly needed in economics and sexuality; in the world of work and in the family.

Our Work Is Holy

We tend to separate our "church life" from our everyday work, family living and leisure time activities. Yet we are called as members of the Church to bring our belief in Jesus into everything we do. That is what is meant by letting him reign over our lives as when we pray "thy kingdom come, thy will be done, on earth as it is heaven."

I think of the work of mothers and fathers, grandparents and extended family members; then the work of farmers, teachers, nurses, employers, sales and service people, office workers, professionals, factory workers, truckdrivers, artists and others. And I think of this prayer given first by a speaker at a recent conference on the laity:

> My work is good work, holy work,
> God's work, the work of the Church.
> Through my work God can
> reign on earth.
> My work is holy. Or can be if I let it.

There is also a paradox here. On one hand, we can forget that life is holy and that our daily activities are the ordinary ways through which God brings salvation into the world. On the other hand, we can think that we are saved through our work, through our efforts alone. No. Salvation is through Jesus Christ. Yet he chooses to use us to make our families holy, to make our work holy, to make our world holy.

In my prayer I was meditating on my tendency to go it alone, to rely on my own activity, my own willfulness.

I really want Jesus to reign over every aspect of my being. I want him to be in charge. But then I want to do it myself.

I am addicted to my own work, that it will save the world, or at least part of it. No, Jesus is the savior. My work, as yours is, is holy work. Still I am only an instrument, a servant, a minister in Jesus' hands.

I am called to teach, not my message, but Jesus' message.

I am called to keep the vision alive—the vision of the Church as the people of God called to build the kingdom in all of society. Again, it is not my vision. It is the vision of Jesus.

I have a tendency to want to do it all myself, to know all the answers. This is a sinful tendency, a pride, an addiction.

So on one hand, I need to know that my work is good, it is God's work and that through it God can reign. All of you do, too.

At the same time, I need to see that the effectiveness of my work depends on God.

Jesus keeps saying to us, "Don't be afraid, I am with you." We are often afraid because we try to go it alone. We forget Jesus.

I keep wondering why I sin. I don't want to. It is always when I go alone, when I forget Jesus. I am powerless without him. This is the healing message of Alcoholics Anonymous.

By letting God reign over every part of our lives, we are made free.

When God reigns over our money, when we give it back to God in thanks and praise, we are free.

When we look upon our use of land as stewards or caretakers rather than absolute owners we are free. When we try to accumulate it, dominate it, possess it, we forget that it belongs to God.

When we can deal with personal conflicts, sickness, grief, family conflict with the message of Jesus as our guide, we are made free.

Yes our daily lives and work are holy. But they need the redeeming presence of Jesus.

Priests

I regularly go to parishes for official two to three day visitations. These visits are among the most important and satisfying things I do all year.

I was spending some time in each classroom of the parish school during a visit. The children asked me how I became a bishop and how I decided to become a priest.

To the first question I replied that Pope Paul VI asked me. I later found out, I told them, that bishops meet regularly to draw up lists of potential candidates for bishop after consulting with priests and other leaders of the diocese. These names are sent to the Holy See through the Pope's representative in Washington.

As to how I decided to become a priest, I told them that I heard the call of God in the ordinary circumstances of my family life. Actually, during a talk that I had with my mother as she was canning tomatoes, I began thinking of studying to be a priest.

As I look back now, it is clear that God had a plan for me and that he called me in such a simple way. My mother said something like "Have you ever thought of becoming a priest?" I knew that I had her prayers and support.

I gradually was able to respond to that call and to give my life to the Lord in the service of his people.

All followers of Christ can look back and see the hand of God in the major choices of their lives. But I want to write especially about priests.

I have known many priests over the years. I know about how God called them each in a different way and that they responded to serve and to give their lives for others. I know their dedication, their many years of preparation, their long hours of work often to the detriment of their health, and their willingness to serve years after most other people retire. They give up the joys of marriage and family.

We are human too. We struggle over the years with sin, discouragement, anxiety and stress. We have to confront pride, greed, lust, dishonesty and all the other temptations that human beings are subject to.

We continually strive through prayer, reading, retreats, spiritual direction and the sacraments to remain true to our commitments.

I felt great pain and deep hurt as I read the recent accusations in the press about sexual abuse and harassment or exploitation by priests.

Only a few years ago such a thing would be hardly mentioned. None of us even imagined that it could happen. We certainly didn't know much about it. But neither did we know much about people with other addictive illnesses such as alcoholism, compulsive eating, workaholism and so forth. We just admonished them to stop, change their lives, use their willpower. We willingly gave them another chance if they showed some signs of improvement.

The evil of the sexual abuse of children, sexual harassment in the workplace, and sexual exploitation of clients by counselors is far more widespread than we ever knew in the past. Church leaders, priests, diocesan and parish staff people are trying to learn more about it.

I am convinced that only a tiny minority of priests are involved. Even one, as we all know, can be the source of so much pain to the victims, their families and to the whole community. Our prayers and love must go out to all of them.

Our prayers and love must go out for the priest too. He offered himself once to the service of God. He must now feel so alone, so wounded, so much in need of support.

There is a second issue about priests which has received a lot of press recently. I refer to the articles about priests who are homosexuals.

First of all it must be clearly said that there is no causal connection between homosexuality and child abuse. They are two separate issues.

Secondly, while I am willing to admit that there are some priests who have homosexual orientation, the numbers are nowhere near the wild, irresponsible and unscientific estimates given in some newspaper reports.

In my limited experience with gay and lesbian people, I have yet to know one who is happy with his or her condition. They look for acceptance, support and understanding. If I learn of a priest with a homosexual orientation I would continue to support him as long as he, like all priests, commits himself to a celibate life.

Pray for priests. Pray for good, dedicated, holy priests. Pray for me that I may be better able to stand with, love and support them.

Liturgy—Especially Music

I was asked once by a national Catholic magazine to list the ten most significant changes that have taken place in the Church during the last twenty-five years. Indeed there have been more changes in the Church during these few years than there have been in the last five hundred.

First on my list were the changes in the liturgy. Nothing touches our everyday lives more than the way in which the Church worships.

Twenty-five years ago the Vatican Council called for a renewal of the liturgy. Rites were to be revised in the light of sound tradition so that they express more clearly the holy things they signify. Full, conscious and active participation by all the faithful was, and still remains, the aim to be considered before all else. "For this is," the Council declared, "the primary and indispensable source from which the faithful are to derive the true Christian spirit."

How are we doing? As I go from parish to parish I see a lot of progress. I am deeply moved as I celebrate diocesan liturgies with attentive, singing, faith-filled people. I feel recharged in body and soul as I worship with parish communities during visitations, confirmations, anniversaries and dedications.

While most people are happy about the changes in the liturgy, there are some who are troubled by them. And there are far too many who are passive. They just do not actively participate.

If before all else the Church wants full and active participation by all the people, then what are some of the things that may help us improve the quality of our worship?

First of all the sacred liturgy has to be seen as central to the life of a Christian. What could be more important in parish life? It therefore needs careful and prayerful preparation. In close cooperation with the parish priest and staff, the parish worship and spiritual life committee meets to pray, study and plan. Well-trained lectors, song leaders, cantors, musicians, artists, servers and ushers all have important roles along with the one who presides.

Because it touches the heart, music has a special place. The most important job of music directors is to direct and encourage *the people* to sing. That means that there should be regular short practices for the assembly. Announcements of hymn numbers should be clear with ample time to find the place. Everyone including the servers and ushers should be encouraged to participate in song. And the song director must be clearly seen by the assembly.

The choir's primary role is to support the active participation in song by the rest of the congregation. The "Gloria," "Holy, Holy," the acclamations and the "Lamb of God" are primarily people's parts. This still gives the choir, cantors, organist and musicians plenty of opportunity to do the more difficult harmonized or polyphonic pieces as meditations, responsories, alternative hymn verses, recessionals and so forth.

While much progress has been made in the congregational singing, I still notice such horrors as little singing in the back half of the Church, choirs alone singing the people's parts, unintelligible announcements, people being asked to sing hymns they don't know, hymns keyed too high, choirs attempting four-part music with insufficient practice.

The Vatican Council called for a reform of the liturgical rites, and the feasts and seasons of the year.

We have all experienced and have been moved by the celebration of the revised rite for confirmation, the liturgy of Christian burial and the Sacred

Triduum of Maundy Thursday, Good Friday and Easter. Many have joined the sick and elderly in the liturgy of the anointing of the sick. Fewer have participated in ordinations to the diaconate and priesthood, the blessing of the holy oils and the dedication of churches.

All of these have enriched our lives and our faith to the extent that we have prepared for them, understood their meaning and opened our hearts to the action of the Holy Spirit.

Retreat, 1988

I remember a television ad of a number of years ago with the punch-line, "I can't believe I ate the whole thing." I don't remember what product was being promoted, but the line stuck and people applied it to different situations.

Well, I ate the whole thing. I just finished making a thirty-day retreat, the Spiritual Exercises of St. Ignatius Loyola, in Guelph, Ontario. I had been thinking about it for a long time.

It was thirty days of complete silence, with a few days to get into the routine of the retreat, and a week to assimilate and process the experience, forty days in all.

When I say complete silence, I mean that. Music was played during the meals. There were no phones, no radios, mail or papers or television. We didn't even nod to, or smile at, another person we passed in the hall. It was thirty days with God.

We had Mass, of course, each day. I prayed my office and rosary. Every day we spent five hour-long periods in prayer, following the directions of St. Ignatius. After each period of contemplation, we took down notes on what happened during our prayer. And then, once a day, we saw our retreat director for thirty to forty minutes, to review our prayer times and what the Lord was saying to us.

The Lord does reveal himself to us, and we can be aware of his presence, his love, and his guidance.

One of the hours of prayer takes place during the middle of the night. The first night I did that I was cold, sat in my chair with wool socks on, and a blanket wrapped around me. It was about 1:00 a.m. I wrote in my notebook: "I think this is stupid. I am tired. I can't focus."

Later, I found that the night time prayers were very productive. I got into the rhythm of the prayer periods. Unbelievable things began to happen.

The whole first week was devoted to contemplations on sin and hell. After five hours a day for six days, believe me, they become real. Toward the end of that, I was really dragging. I felt depressed, desolate and wrung out. But then I came to experience God's love for me, a deep awareness and acknowledgement of my sins, a heartfelt sorrow and a clear knowledge that Jesus has forgiven all my sins.

The special grace asked for and received during this retreat was an intimate and personal knowledge of Jesus. This came through the contemplation of the second week. In my prayer, I found myself with Jesus. I talked with him and I listened to him. I began to discern what the Lord wants me to do as I minister in the Diocese of New Ulm these next fifteen years. I came to some clear directions and decisions. I discussed them with my director. Together we worked out a plan for some specific actions that I will take in my life. I believe that they are decisions guided by the Spirit of God.

The third week is devoted to the Passion and Death of Jesus. I was given the grace really to accompany Jesus in his passion. I knew he was suffering for me and I learned more about what it means to serve. The fourth week was devoted to the Resurrection and the appearances of the Risen Lord. With it came a deep realization that Jesus lives. I experienced hours of prayer, totally carried away in the contemplation of these mysteries.

This has been a once in a life time experience. It has changed my life. I prayed for you all—priests, pastoral administrators and diocesan staff members by name, each individual parish, my parents, my family, my aunts, uncles, my cousins, relatives, teachers, friends, and all of the people that God has put in my life.

In one of my prayer periods, I prayed about God's personal and intimate love for me. I share with you what I wrote in my notebook:

Jesus, you were there, you touched me, you loved me when... (I went through my whole life.)

You were there when I was in my mother's womb.

You were there when I grew up in a loving home:
- in my high school years
- when I went to the seminary
- in many of my teachers
- when I was ordained
- when I came to know the meaning of friendship

You were there when I was teaching:
- when I went to Rome during the Vatican Council
- when I experienced a personal faith in you
- when I knew your love
- when I went to St. Austin's parish
- when I was ordained a bishop and spoke of my faith.

Jesus, you were there when I sinned:
- when I forgot you
- when I turned against you.

You were there in my sickness, and in my weakness.

Jesus, Savior, you were there, you touched me, you loved me,
- when I preached in your name
- when I celebrated the Eucharist
- when I received the sacraments
- when you forgave me
- when I suffered rejection and hurts from others.

Today, during this moment of prayer, you are here, you love me, you touch me. O Jesus, I love you, I adore you, I praise you.

A Motley Crew

The passion, death and resurrection of Jesus have a new meaning for me this year. One day I meditated on the disciples of Jesus. They had been with Jesus for the better part of three years. They had followed him, listened to him, ate with him, and watched his many miracles. Yet, when the chips were down, most of them abandoned him.

What came through to me was that we are so much like them. Many of us go through the motions of following Jesus. Our names are on the parish register. Our Christian observance is often external. When there is a time for a real decision, so often we abandon him.

At the arrest in the garden, Judas betrayed him with a kiss. Peter and John followed at a distance to the high priest's house. John used his influence to get the favor of allowing Peter to come in to the courtyard. Peter was so compulsive, so generous. But, when confronted by a servant girl, when challenged, he denied Jesus. We can do that too. We don't want to be counted. We blend in with the culture of our day.

The rest of the disciples ran away. That can happen to us too. When the going gets tough, we compromise, we remain silent, we fail to stick our neck out, we go along with the system.

On the Way of the Cross, some women were unafraid and came forward to identify themselves with Jesus. The women of Jerusalem wept, and were comforted by Jesus. Tradition has it that Veronica helped him, was rewarded by a "true icon" of Jesus, and that Mary, his mother, suffered with him on the Way of the Cross. Simon the Cyrenean, at first coerced to carry the cross, later, we are told, became a disciple.

Mary and John stood under the cross. In Mark's Gospel, only the women from Galilee remained with Jesus.

The thief, Dismas, by confessing his faith in Jesus, was rewarded with eternal life.

Only two well known leaders came forth and publicly identified themselves as followers of Jesus. Joseph, a member of the Sanhedrin, and Nicodemus, a Pharisee who came to him at night, took Jesus down from the cross and laid him in the tomb.

Not much of a crowd. The ones who ran away, the ones who denied him, the ones who betrayed him, the ones who were coerced into following him, the thieves, those outside, the faithful few, men and women, who remained with him. This is what the church is made of, a motley crew. We can be identified with them.

Even after the Resurrection, the disciples were still confused, still afraid. They didn't quite know what to do. People didn't believe them when they said they had seen the Lord. Sometimes, they were not too sure of themselves.

Still, they stuck together. Jesus appeared to them in the upper room at the shore of the lake. He came to be with them, to support them. He prepared breakfast for them. Overjoyed, they declared, "It is the Lord."

But it wasn't until the Holy Spirit came upon them that they really began to boldly proclaim their faith in Jesus.

What came to me so clearly in my meditation was how much we are like the disciples. So human, so afraid. Until we are touched and moved by the Holy Spirit.

I too have experienced the presence of the Risen Lord. He has forgiven me. He has consoled me. He has given me direction. He has spoken to me.

He continues to support me, feed me, encourage me.

That is what the Resurrection is all about. Jesus lives! He is still among us. He shows us his love. He gives us his peace.

God bless you all.